How To Give Birth
To A God

The Honorable Minister Louis Farrakhan

D1598220

EDITOR'S NOTE

This book is comprised from edited excerpts from the "How to Give Birth to A God" lecture series delivered by the Honorable Minister Louis Farrakhan on the following dates:

Part 1	*July 26, 1987*
Part 2	*July 29, 1987*
Part 3	*August 2, 1987*
Part 4	*August 5, 1987*
Part 5	*August 10, 1987*

CONTENTS

PART III: REFORMATION

PART IV: ELEVATION

PART V: TRANSFORMATION

FOREWORD

My subject is dedicated to Barbara Antia and it is dedicated to all the Sisters and really dedicated to my dear Brothers.

I have been working on this subject for over 15 years. I am so proud of this series of lectures that if I died tonight, I would feel that I have done my job.

If you get this series of lectures, I do not need to ever talk again, for what is in these lectures, which I will condense for you today, be it the Will of Allah (God), will be enough for you to get up out of this condition totally, completely, and forever.

The Honorable Minister Louis Farrakhan

August 1987

I
PREPARATION

1

A Strong Family Produces a Strong Nation

If there is no strong family, there can be no strong people or nation. In the holy world in the East, the punishment of death passes upon the adulterer and fornicator. In the Bible, Allah (God) gave Moses a strong law. Moses was not only a law-giver. He was also a nation-builder and civilization-builder. To build a civilization, there must be a strong law to protect women, family, and the institution of marriage.

The punishment Moses set for adultery was stoning the guilty party to death because the violation of the word, commitment, and vow that one spouse made to the other spouse in the Presence of God is a violation of the upward journey toward God. When a wife has relations with a strange man or a husband has relations with a strange woman, it is a violation of marital vows and breaks the family. If it breaks the family and scatters the husband and wife, it damages and makes the children insecure.

When the family has broken apart, many consequences follow. If we want a strong people and a strong nation, then we must produce strong men and women with a strong commitment to each other through the institution of marriage.

The Honorable Elijah Muhammad wanted us to marry. He taught us that Almighty God Allah says in the Holy Qur'an that He hates divorce. There was a time in the Catholic Church when a member would get excommunicated for getting a divorce. Today, men and women marry as though marriage is a pastime or a joke.

Our word to each other and our word to God are not serious. We do not have any real commitment.

When we say, "for better or worse," we really mean "only for the better." When we say, "in sickness and in health," we really mean "only in health." When we say, "for richer or poorer," we really mean "you better have some money, honey." When we say, "until death us do part," we really mean "until the death of this marriage, then we will part." We do not have any commitment to longevity. We enter marriage with the thought of ending it if it does not work. We enter marriage with the thought that we will not commit ourselves to fight to make it work.

By not taking our commitment to marriage seriously, we do not take the commitment to the journey of life toward Allah (God) seriously. Prophet Muhammad (peace be upon him) said, "Marriage is one-half of faith." If marriage is one-half of faith, then marriage is one-half of our journey to God. In Arabic, the word for marriage is *nikah*, which means "to unite."

When marital vows are spoken, it does not mean that the husband and wife are united. It means that they have made a commitment to struggle for the unity of two souls, two independent beings, and two independent essences that come from one Originator. Marriage is a struggle to unite.

Any goal of value presents a difficulty factor to attain. The difficulty factor in life means that Allah (God) must have created us to face the difficulty, not turn our backs or run from the difficulty. God has brought us into a difficult life and given us the wherewithal, with His Help, to overcome all obstacles that lie in the pathway of our progress toward Him.

Marriage is a part of the journey because we do not know who and what we are without marriage. This is why the Holy Qur'an does not condone being a monk or a nun. God has not demanded celibacy from you. In neither the Bible nor the Holy Qur'an has He

5

instructed men to be eunuchs. He has not asked the Pope to take a vow that he will not touch a woman. He has not asked the Father or the Cardinal to take a vow that they will not touch a woman, even though they ache so to do—and do.

God has not asked a woman to take a vow not to have a man because our growth and development as human beings are connected to the struggle to overcome the difficulty factor in uniting the male with the female and the female with the male. Any man who denies himself that joy and pleasure and that struggle and pain denies himself a part of the journey toward God Himself.

Any man who would walk away from a woman who has nurtured his babies and taken care of him is a man who would walk away from God. He is a man who would walk away from his commitment to the Divine Being when things get rough. We can tell how faithful a person will be to God by how faithful that person is to little things—and marriage is not a little thing. It is a big thing in the eyes of God.

2
You Build Your Own World

Marriage is a trial, at best. It starts beautifully, full of love, tenderness, and service between the husband and wife. But after a short while, the couple becomes familiar with each other, and their words turn cold. They begin to learn things about each other that they did not know before. How are you going to handle it?

The Bible tells a parable of a man going forth sowing seeds. Some of the seeds fell on stony ground. Some fell by the wayside. Some were planted deep in fertile soil. The sower is Jesus bringing truth, and the field is the hearts of men. Some men receive the seed with joy, but eventually, an evil one comes and steals it from them.

So many people are happy on the day they get married. All the guests say the husband and wife look beautiful, and they buy expensive gifts for the couple. But six months later, the gifts are hardly worn out while the marriage is already worn out. Your marriage is worn out before the dishes break. Your marriage is worn out before the coffee percolates in the pot. Your marriage is worn out because you never intended to make your word bond and thereby bring forth life. So, marriage is a trial.

Like the parable of the sower of the seed, some people receive marriage with joy. But by and by, the cares of the world choke out their word, and it becomes unprofitable. Some people get married and, at first, there is bliss. When you see one spouse, you see the other. When you see the other spouse, you see the one. But by and by, when you see one, you never see the other; and when you see the other, you never see the one. When they are together, they look like they are in strain and pain with each other. The cares of the world have choked out the word they have given to each other. Their marriage becomes unprofitable. Eventually, abuse develops: the woman abuses herself; the man abuses himself, and he abuses the woman.

Battered women are not a phenomenon in the world. Men have become so cold and callous and filled with a lack of understanding of life that they crush their women. They cannot cope with the minds of their women when they argue, so they beat their women down with their fists as though they were beating men. Women are battered and live in homes with men who claim to love them. Yet every day, fisticuffs break out between them. The man beats the woman to the point that the woman is fearful for her life.

How can women live in fear in a home and produce the right kind of offspring? How can they live under that kind of tyranny and produce children who recognize love, justice, mercy, and

7

tenderness? Women are producing wicked children because they live under environmental circumstances that make them able to produce a devil.

Men abuse their wives and children. Men do not set a just rule in their homes or do justice by their children, while at the same time, they condemn the White man for ruling by a law that favors White people and disfavors Black people. In judging our children, we play favorites. Some of us prefer the lighter-complexioned children rather than the darker. We favor the lighter and suppress the darker. Some of us favor the girl rather than the boy or the boy rather than the girl. We openly show favoritism to the girl to the detriment of the boy or vice versa. We all have our favorites. We all have our unjust dealings in the home, not realizing, thinking, contemplating, or taking a second thought about the consequences of the injustice we are setting up.

"You build your own world," the Honorable Elijah Muhammad taught. "You can make it a heaven for yourself, or you can make it a hell. Heaven and hell," he said, "are two conditions of life. You can make either one." We have a responsibility for the condition of our lives. We cannot simply blame it on the White man. We are either willing agents of the White man in our destruction or willing agents of God in our reconstruction.

What are you doing when you batter yourself? What are you doing when you abuse yourself? How can a woman bear a good child for a man while he is beating her? How do you treat your wife when she is pregnant with your life? What do you think about her as she grows fuller with your life? How do you handle her mind, not her body? Mothers, how do you handle yourselves?

The time to prepare for motherhood and fatherhood is when you are a child. A mother has a heavy responsibility. Fathers do, too, but it does not equal the responsibility of a mother and a woman in any way.

8

The Honorable Elijah Muhammad made it against the law for a Brother to strike his wife. He put us out of the society of the mosque for 90 days for the first offense and six months for the second offense because it is tremendously wrong for a man to beat a woman. The Honorable Elijah Muhammad taught us, "When you teach a man, you teach an individual, but when you teach a woman, you teach a nation." So, when you beat a man, you beat an individual, but when you beat a woman, you beat a nation. We must think about our actions and the consequences thereof. God forbids the beating of our wives and the abuse of ourselves.

What are the young men and women doing with themselves? The sign of being a man today is that you must smoke and drink. If you do not smoke or drink in this society, you are not considered a real man. If the amount of cigarettes you smoke and alcohol you drink is a sign of manhood, why didn't God give us a mother with breasts that distill whiskey to her infants rather than milk? With each puff inhaled of a cigarette, at least 4,000 different chemicals enter our bodies. These include toxic hydrogen cyanide, carbon monoxide, nitrogen dioxide gases, and four dozen compounds such as benzopyrene and radioactive plutonium 210.

All are known carcinogens. These chemical vapors and tobacco smoke get deposited in the mouth, nose, throat, and lungs. These organs become coated with burnt plant resins called tar, in which lies most of the cancer-inducing potential of tobacco smoke.

Most chronic heavy drinkers typically also smoke. When smokers become thirsty, they wash down the cigarette smoke coating in their mouths and throat with whiskey, wine, or beer. Alcohol is not, by itself, a carcinogen. Still, it may act as a solvent, dissolving the tar-trapped tobacco poisons and easing the transport of carcinogens across the membranes of the body. The smoker continues to drink. Soon, he lights another cigarette and inhales deeply.

Meanwhile, behind his embattled lungs, his liver has gone on full alert to save his life. This three-pound chemical factory, called the liver, cleans most toxins from the bloodstream, reacts to alcohol as a foreign substance, and metabolizes 95 percent of it into other chemicals. When turning its energy to clearing half an ounce of pure alcohol—the amount in a standard drink—per hour from the blood of a drinker and smoker, the liver's other metabolic functions suffer a sharp decrease.

Since the liver is supposed to clear toxins from our body, every time you put alcohol in your system, the liver is on alert and goes to work to cleanse your system of this poison. Because this sharply decreases its function of clearing other poisons from your body, the drinker and smoker continue to build up toxins until their bodies become a toxic waste dump site on a path to death.

While battling alcohol, the liver puts aside another important function, clearing fat from the bloodstream. Excess fatty substances, called lipids and fat by-products, begin clogging the bloodstream. At the same time, chemicals from cigarette smoke increase the coagulating tendency of the blood. Thickening blood begins to clog the capillaries, and blood cells carrying food and oxygen struggle to reach the cells of the body.

Young smokers and drinkers are still producing sperm and eggs that will one day become our future and the future of life on the earth. Young women are producing eggs that are already deficient. Young men are producing sperm that are already deficient. This deficient sperm is going to contact a deficient egg. No wonder we cannot live to 100 years without our bodies falling apart, while the old patriarchs lived 500 to 900 years. It is not that God is against you; you are against God in your lifestyle.

What are the effects of this lifestyle on a pregnant woman? If a man already beats her, she carries her baby while being filled with bitterness. Pregnant women should understand that when alcohol and tobacco are present together, they perform a synergistic function, according to medical scientists. By themselves, they are bad for the body. When both are present, they increase the toxic potential of each other in their synergistic function. When a pregnant woman smokes, she inhales carbon monoxide. Nicotine is in your blood, and your blood oxygen-carrying capacity is going to the fetus, which depends on it. It's now taken over by that carbon monoxide.

Women legislate or give death to their children while carrying them in the womb. Men who use crack or heroin transmit these drugs in their bloodstream. If it is in their bloodstream, then it is in their testicles. When they manufacture sperm—the new life of you that will go on after you—are dead. You have already sentenced your babies to death before they are even born into the world. This is the reason ignorance is a curse. We can talk about the White man, but our ignorance is our worst enemy. If we do not impart knowledge to our people, we who have it will be punished by Allah (God) for keeping such knowledge from a sleeping, ignorant people.

Crack, cocaine, heroin, and alcohol affect the sperm and the egg. A defective egg has been fertilized by a defective sperm. The defective sperm and egg try to get a grip in a defective womb because the chemists of this world have women putting into themselves chemicals, the nature of which they do not know or understand. The chemicals weaken the walls of the uterus so that the newly fertilized egg cannot get a firm grip in the womb. This is a cause of many miscarriages.

Women are poisoned and feed poison to their children, which causes the debilitation or weakening of their children's brainpower. Women are weakening their children's physical structure, the structural base, by what they put in their mouths and systems. Girls should begin tending to themselves to prepare to do the most sacred thing a woman can do. Feminists may question what sacredness when compared to the various professions that women work in today. Women are chemists, doctors, lawyers, teachers, and typists. But for whom are they working? What kind of business are they running? What business is more important than the business of human life and a better humanity coming on this planet?

This is why the Honorable Elijah Muhammad set up the Muslim Girls in Training and General Civilization Class. One of the seven training units teaches women how to rear their children because women know how to do everything else except bring a decent child on the planet to have the mental strength of a giant, a prophet, and a seer. Women have the capacity to bring giants onto this earth but bringing a giant onto the earth is not an accident. Women have the capacity to birth a god on the scene.

3
The Force to Change Reality

There is an old maxim: "The hand that rocks the cradle rules the world." What is wrong with the world today is that there are no strong men in it, which is connected to the condition of women. We do not have any giant thinkers among us and hardly any courageous men willing to stand up against the odds and deliver our people from our oppressor. Cowardly men are a disservice to women. When the going gets tough, they back down and weaken.

There are no strong men in the world to take charge of the destiny of our people because women have been weakened and destroyed. Women do not know how to produce a strong man. It is not that women do not have the potential or capacity. It is that women do not have the knowledge. Because they do not know how to do what they are born into the world to do, they miss their task. Children are born into the world out of lust and passion, without any thought and planning on the part of their parents.

The force to change the reality of the way we live is correct knowledge deposited in the right place. With careful planning, proper decisions, and choices, along with the continued application of desire, effort, and will, women can produce mental giants. Women can produce a god. The woman may not do it herself in terms of the manifestation of such power, but the woman is the womb through which that power comes.

That is why to abuse a woman is to abuse the womb of God. If the world is in need of great and honorable men of vision and right action, women are going to have to produce that kind of man. Women today, whom God will bless, lay down and dream of becoming the mothers of great men who would make a difference. That is nothing to be ashamed of.

What about the women who have never had that dream? They are of producing age with eggs that can be fertilized but whose minds have never conceived the thought of producing a child that would change the direction of their people. What kind of baby will they produce? Their pregnancies are accidents waiting to happen. Why don't more women think like that? Precisely because women have never been taught or trained about the magnificence of who they are.

Some people may say that I appear to favor women when I teach. It is because I was made wise from the cradle by my mother. Someone was going to have to come to free the woman. Someone was going to have to come to put the woman in the right state and frame of mind and give her the right frame of reference from which she could draw power to make a change. That person was the Honorable Elijah Muhammad. I was so in tune with my father, the Honorable Elijah Muhammad, that if 75 percent of his work is with the woman, why should I not lean in the direction that is the heaviest part of his work if I am his student and helper? The scholars who write about Jesus call him "the desire of women." This has many meanings, but scholars say it means that women in the nation of oppressed Jews wanted to produce the Deliverer. Each woman wanted or desired to possess the womb God would bless with the Deliverer. So, Jesus was the desire of women.

4
The Life of a Pregnant Woman Prepares Her Child's Mind

A woman cannot produce a god if the desire is absent. The thought of how to produce a god must develop before the conception of a child. Before a woman has a baby, she must prepare her body and mind for what will ultimately become a reality in her life. Boys must prepare themselves to father powerful sperm. Sperm is not fathered by the act of sexual intercourse alone. Sperm is fathered by the thought present in the brain, which empowers sperm by becoming the force in the head of the sperm, which will finally germinate and fertilize the egg.

We cannot be mindless and produce mental giants, although it happens accidentally. But if you think about what you are and who you are, you can do it every time. Because of the condition of our people, we do not want to hit and miss. We want to produce a giant. Every time the womb opens, let a god come forth.

This is why the White man is so afraid today. The birth rate of White people is decreasing while the birth rate of Black people is increasing. Even though everything is against Black people chemically and biologically, we still produce children who have great power. Even though we may birth them into nothing but negative circumstances, the child still develops a will to overcome the negative circumstances.

We must consider several factors. Living a natural life, which means a life in harmony with the laws of nature, is preparation for giving birth to a god. It must be a life not given to alcohol, cigarettes, or drugs because the synergism of such intoxicants has devastating effects on our brain cells, bloodstream, and sperm or eggs. There is a saying: "Turn me on. Come on, baby, light my fire." Sister, you have a fire. Properly turning on a woman is the most sacred function of a man. If a woman is turned on properly, a natural love springs from her, which is absolutely and vitally necessary for the proper preparation of a mental giant.

The woman has the impressive ability to impress on the mind of the growing child in her womb, like the mind is a blank piece of paper. She can write on the brain while the brain is forming. It is dangerous to play with women. It is dangerous for women not to know how valuable they are because they can become ignorant tools to be abused rather than properly used for the service of God.

The Honorable Elijah Muhammad said, *"Where there are no decent women, there are no decent men, for the woman is the Mother of Civilization."* The Honorable Elijah Muhammad said, *"No nation can rise any higher than its woman."*

A woman can impress her inner desires on the child that is forming in her womb. Just like she can kill them by forming them from the smoke she inhales and the foods she eats, she can also make them with the thoughts she thinks. That is why a woman's mind has to be guarded by a man. If there is no man, the woman must perform the duty herself, walk her post in a perfect manner, and take charge of her post. She must keep alert and observe everything within sight or hearing that will damage her mind because her mind is the laboratory that produces the new world.

A woman's prayers from the depth of her heart, crying out to Allah (God), impress themselves on her child's brain. The stronger and more continuous her thoughts are, they can resemble a printing press that stamps an impression on the mind of the forming fetus. The body and mind are like blank pieces of paper on which mothers are the first to write. Whatever they write is permanent. This is why the scholars consider women to be God's assistants or co-creators with God.

The life led by a pregnant woman is the preparation of the mind for her child. Her thoughts and desires stamp the mind, like writing on paper. Although unseen, what she is making after it is writ, she cannot take back what she has produced. Only God can put His Hand over her destructive work and bring good out of a life prepared for death.

Thought, desire, and will are key elements. Thought, desire, and will have the power to impress the forming child with the power of good or evil. Parents are responsible for properly preparing themselves for parenthood, but it must begin before conception. But who cares? Who is concerned? No one teaches this. No one makes young people responsible for the destruction of their bodies and minds. Who cares? Muhammad does.

We are responsible not only for preparing ourselves for parenthood. We are also responsible for arranging the proper conditions and environment, called prenatal development. We are responsible for living properly regarding rest, food, exercise, and especially the proper mental attitudes that conquer emotional stresses. We are responsible for recognizing that impressions during pregnancy shape the destiny of the offspring for good or evil and for the good and future of the nation as a whole.

When a man finds out about the unexpected pregnancy of a woman, curses her, and then abandons her, how does the woman react? She becomes afraid to tell her parents. Her friends may suggest getting an abortion or doing things to cause a miscarriage. When someone questions if she is pregnant, she may lie and deny the life forming in her womb. She has become a liar and a murderer. Lying and murder happen in the darkness surrounding the womb while women are fashioning life, and we wonder why our children are liars and murderers today. We are replicating the history of the making of the White man on the island of Pelan.

The Honorable Elijah Muhammad taught us the history of Yakub and how the devil was made. When Yakub got his followers on the island of Pelan, every laborer who worked to form the White race was a liar and a murderer. Lying and murder were in the nature of the children they produced. Why did Elijah Muhammad teach that history? He taught it so we could know that every time a baby is in the womb, the woman is secreted away on her own special island. She can make her child a liar, murderer, and devil or make her child a god.

The power of the Brown germ and Black germ is in the womb. It is manifested in the negative and positive qualities of the child. If you want a positive child, you must eliminate the negative. If you feed and graft on the negative and kill the positive, you will produce a negative result: a murderer, a liar, and a child born with the propensity to kill. It will kill its own parents. It will rob and deceive its own parents. Regardless of color, White or Black, this is the nature of the womb.

The White man is born into the world a liar and a murderer. Jesus said, "I beheld your father when he fell from heaven. He was a liar from the beginning and abode not in the truth. He was a murderer and the lust of your father, you shall do." How did Jesus know him? Jesus knew him from the womb and how he was formed. Therefore, Jesus knew his nature.

That is why the White man can't help himself. He is a liar and a murderer. He has wreaked more havoc on the earth than any other people in the annals of history because of the circumstances surrounding his making on the island of Pelan, or Patmos as it is called in the Bible. This history teaches us the value of a woman and her womb. Whatever happens in and around a woman while she is fashioning life helps form the nature of the child.

Many women hate the fact that they are pregnant when they find out. They become embittered that the man made them pregnant. They reject the life forming inside them. They cannot accept the fact that their beautiful shapes will change. They value the shape of their bodies more than the shape of their minds. They hate the child because the father did not turn on the natural wellspring of their love. Since they did not want to be pregnant, it was an accident that resulted from passion. This hatred leads to murder. The thoughts that a woman impresses upon the child are, "I do not want you. I do not like you. I wish to destroy you."

When the child comes into the world, the child does not realize why it has feelings of self-rejection. No one can tell them something good about themselves without thinking that person is playing a game on them. It is because their mothers rejected them in the womb. Even though they grow up, they continue to practice self-rejection and self-hatred and subtly become murderers of their own selves. That is why we engage in self-destructive habits in the name of having a good time.

We get drunk: Killing ourselves. We get high: Killing ourselves. We do not have any value in our own eyes, so it is very difficult for another person to get us to see and put value on ourselves. We are potential murderers or bombs ready to explode. Small conflicts cause us to become ready to fight and kill one another. We are marked with vileness and bitterness.

That is why we can indulge our minds with songs that are filthy and commit acts that are low down. We were conceived with low-down, filthy thoughts from the passion of adultery, lust, fornication, and debauchery. It must be generally accepted that, if there is to be a real reformation of the world, if ever the millennium of purity, chastity, righteousness, peace, and justice is to be achieved on this earth, it will result from correctly, wisely, and rationally directed parental laws. It will result from mothers who understand that they are co-creators with God. They are God's assistants in creating a better world.

5
The Power of Will and Thought

Where there are no decent women, there can never be any decent men. Where women are hurled down, men can never be lifted up. The destiny of the individual, the destiny of the race, and the destiny of the nation depend upon the mother and prenatal conditions arranged for her child.

If the developmental propagation of the species is undertaken knowingly and understandingly, father and mother, working harmoniously with each other, can do more to foster the reforms so urgently needed in the world than all social institutions combined. No reform school, prison, or penal institution can reform lives. There must be a special redemption and a special redeemer to undertake the reformation of lives that have been made wrong.

If true to her feminine nature, the woman is really advanced over the man, not because of her beauty, accomplishments, or even the nature of her love when correctly awakened, but because she possesses the womb. The womb is the laboratory wherein are fashioned those who will inhabit the world, where the woman co-operates with or is an assistant to Allah (God) in the formation, reformation, and final completion of the human being.

There is no reformation without the reform of women. How do you reform something that has been rejected from birth? It is a good thing that God has given us the nature to submit and the nature to rebel. If I did not rebel against the circumstances into which I was born, I could never be what I am today.

My mother tried to kill me when I was a baby in her womb because she did not know what she was carrying. She regrets that desire to this day, and she tells me, as she goes into the valley of death, that she begs the pardon of God for trying to kill the life in her womb. She marked me with her thinking, and this is what led to my fall from the Honorable Elijah Muhammad.

Even though the Honorable Elijah Muhammad told me so many good things about myself, I could not believe them because my mother rejected me in her womb. Rejection in the womb leads not to self-denial but self-negation. When you get older, you cannot accept yourself. You do not love or want yourself, so you easily become somebody else. That is why we can call ourselves Cuban, Mexican, Arab, or anybody else except who we are. We reject ourselves.

I thank Allah (God) that a Wise God put His Hand over a mother who, though good and wonderful in her ignorance, set a mark on her child. But Allah (God) said, "No, I am going to give him the will to overcome his mother and her thinking when she was forming him in her womb. I am going to give him the will to say, 'I rebel against that!'" As a child, no matter what she said, I said, "I'll show her. The world will respect me one day."

Because I was determined to overcome the circumstances of my birth, I am where I am by the Help of God. What about you? You cannot give up on life and say, "I had a bad circumstance. My poor mother did not want me. I'm this way in the world, so I'll commit suicide," and walk around in the street with your head down like you cannot make a difference or change reality.

Will and thought can reverse the whole process. A new thought can rearrange our genetic structure. That is why God says, "I make all things new." How we relate to circumstances surrounding our pregnancy determines certain character traits in the child. This is called prenatal influence.

Eve was given to Adam. The serpent deceived Eve to eat his teaching, styled in the Bible as the forbidden fruit, and to feed it to Adam. They fell and then had children. The duality is present. God made them good, while Satan made them depart from good. Then they produced children: Cain and Abel, two children with two different dispositions, coming out of the same womb.

We cannot consistently produce giants from our wombs. Instead, we hit and miss. We produce a good child, then four bad ones. We produce a good one, a really bad one, another good one, another really bad one, and then a mediocre one, followed by a degenerate, then a good one.

In the Bible, Eve produces Cain and Abel, two brothers with different characteristics from the same womb. One of them has tenderness and a heart for God. He was conceived when Adam was in his right mind, so that right mind was part of Abel's conception. The next time, Cain was produced. When Cain saw Abel achieving, he became jealous of Abel. Envy leads to hatred, which then leads to murder. Cain murders his righteous brother and covers him up.

That happens every day. The seed of good and evil is in us, but when the good tries to come up, the evil of ourselves, which developed because of the thoughts that went into our make-up, we crush out and bury the good in ourselves. We kill our Brother and bury him.

On the world scene today, when a messenger or prophet is raised, he brings the best and worst out of us at the same time. Those who follow the prophet try to better their lives. Those who hate the prophet and are jealous of the prophet's success raise a group of people that they infect with their poison against the prophet. At the root of their hatred is envy. At the root of that envy is the thought that went into their formation when they were being made.

6
Circumcision of the Heart is Necessary

Jesus said, "It is not the circumcision of the foreskin of the penis, but it is the circumcision of the heart." When you circumcise the penis, you cut off the foreskin, which hides debris in a dark and damp place, which causes the multiplication of bacteria. To clean an uncircumcised penis, you must pull back the foreskin. Otherwise, during the act of procreation, a dirty mass of bacteria will be injected into the woman. Even as the life germ is injected, death-causing bacteria will be injected at the same time.

What does that mean on a spiritual or metaphysical level? It means that someone with a heart that preaches the Word of God out of envy, jealousy, and hatred for his Brother has a heart that is corroded with disease. When the Word of God comes out of that person's mouth, poison comes out with the Word and contaminates it.

We must speak the Word of God with the hope in our hearts that the Word will regenerate life in people and continue to elevate them through that life. The hearts of those who speak must be washed with prayers, hopes, and aspirations toward purity so that they keep cleaning their hearts and God keeps helping them to clean their hearts.

In the Holy Qur'an, Allah (God) says, "Arise and warn, thy Lord do magnify, thy garments do purify and uncleanness do shun." If we do not purify our hearts from hatred, malice, bitterness, and resentment, we will create a womb that will produce children after our warped, hateful, and bitter articulation of the Word of God.

This is why we, in the Nation of Islam, had to grow up. You cannot preach the Word of God with a heart filled with hatred for the White man. Allah (God) says He is The Beneficent and The Merciful. Whenever hatred enters our communication, we raise children from that emotion, which absolutely poisons the Word of God. People cannot see the Word of God in its proper dimension simply because we, the speakers of it, are immature in our representation of The Beneficent.

The wicked one who is here is only here by the Permission of God. When you see the wicked one and hate him and desire to kill him, all your negative thoughts come out in your words. Therefore, you poison the Word itself. This is why the Messenger of God said, "It is expedient for you that I go away." In other words, "I have taught you and given you a base, but I am going away now so that you can grow up into that word and a mature expression of that word."

Mary is elevated to a very high position in the Bible and Christian theology. The Catholic Church recites a prayer, in part: "Holy Mary, Mother of God, pray for us sinners, now and at the hour of our death. Holy Mary, blessed art thou among women and blessed is the fruit of thy womb, Jesus."

Islamic scholars and teachers, based upon the Holy Qur'an, reject the exaltation of Mary to a position of worship. And they are right. But in rejecting that aspect of Christology, they also reject the wisdom contained in it, which has only been exaggerated and put out of proper context. Islamic scholars and teachers go to the extreme by not only rejecting Mary, the mother of God but in rejecting womanhood.

In the Holy Qur'an, God communicated through an angel to Mary when she was a girl. Allah (God) says to Mary, *"I am only a* bearer of a message of thy Lord: that I will give you a pure boy." Mary said, *"How can I have a son and no mortal has yet touched me, nor have I been unchaste?"* He said, *"So (it will be). Thy Lord says: It is easy to Me; and that We may make him a sign to men and a mercy from Us. And it is a matter decreed."* After God told Mary, in advance, that she was going to give birth to a pure boy, she drew aside from her family and screened herself from them in preparation for the child she was going to bring into the world.

Mary is a woman who must be studied. The 19th Chapter of the Holy Qur'an is entitled "Maryam" because the number 19 is the secret number that unfolds the secret of God. To understand the secret of God, you must understand Mary and the womb. Mary and Elizabeth are two women mentioned in the Bible and Holy Qur'an. Elizabeth was the mother of John, and Mary was the mother of Jesus. They are related. One is six months older than the other. There is a lot of wisdom in this. The father was instructed for the birth of John, and the mother was instructed for the birth of Jesus. Although Elizabeth was a woman who grew up in the temple, Mary was a woman who grew up under the Law of Moses.

In the Holy Qur'an, Allah (God) says to Zacharias, "This boy, there never was a boy like him before. He is going to be a good one." Zacharias was not going to become pregnant and carry him. Elizabeth was going to carry him in her womb. So, she had to be a good woman, with a good thought in her mind, to produce that kind of child for God. Mary had to be a phenomenal woman. She said, "My soul doth magnify and glorify the Lord." The very essence of Mary is that she was God-fearing.

According to scholars, the brain of a child is fashioned by the thoughts, desires, and blood of the mother. She makes brain. She makes brawn. Men should understand why we should be careful how we handle women. Women are making the brain of our future. Mary is called "the Mother of God." That is not wrong.

That is right. David says in Psalms, "Ye are all gods, children of the Most High God." Proverbs reads, "A wise child maketh a glad father, but a foolish child is the heaviness of its mother." The Bible also says, "Train up the child in the way it should go and, when it is old, it will not depart from thee." Then, the trainer, teacher, shaper, and molder is the mother.

What is in mothers will be in their children. Since mothers make the brains of their children, what do their brains constantly think about while they are producing new life? Is it soap operas and all the negative shows on television? It is better to turn off the television while a woman is pregnant. They should not go to the movies where actors are cursing or watch movies that make them cry or where they are watching death, murder, and mayhem.

The White man has committed crimes against humanity when he commits a crime against a woman. A crime against a woman is a crime against humanity. A crime against a woman is almost an unpardonable sin because it destroys a co-operator with God in the procreation of human life.

It requires a great woman to become a superior mother. In many respects, most truly great men resemble their mothers in temperament and adaptability. The quality of a great woman is not that she has a lot of force and power over a man. The quality of a great woman is that she loves deeply and unselfishly. The quality of a great woman is that she serves with joy. The quality of a great woman is that she feels good as a sweetheart, a good wife, a good mother, a good grandmother, and a real companion to her husband. Above all the great qualities of a woman, the greatest quality is love. This is why Mary is exalted and called the mother of God. If a woman knows how to mother, she can produce a child in the image and likeness of God.

As women get themselves ready, the first thing they must do is weed out their garden and pluck up the characteristics, thoughts, and habits that will not be good for their child to feed on—bitterness, envy, jealousy, hatred, and vile behaviors that come from vile thoughts. Women must make a sacrifice and rid themselves of these negativities if they want to produce a child for God. Women must clean up their bodies.

Cast away the cigarette. Cast away the alcohol. Cast away the crack, dope, pills, and other unnecessary drugs. Women must stop allowing someone else to cook their meals, especially pre-packaged meals with a lot of chemical preservatives. If women are going to make a child, they must begin by purifying their bodies, which will receive the seed of life. Women must prepare their physical womb and the womb of their minds—both wombs work together, co-operating with God for the resuscitation, reformation, regeneration, and procreation of human life.

7
Fostering an Atmosphere of Love

Women must make a serious choice for a man. A woman should not run around having sex with every man who asks but should examine a man's mind to see whether he is worthy of her because what you see is just about what you get. When a woman is about to conceive, she should plan for the child because she is sick of the world and what the world has produced.

If a man wants a better life, he should warm up the love in his wife by treating her like she is the co-operator with God. She is our future. She is our connection to the future. When a husband tells his wife that he loves her, he is saying, "I love the future." When he handles her right, he is saying, "I love my future. I am handling my future right." When he is kind to her, he is kind to his future. When he is loving to her, he is loving to his future.

When they decide it is time to produce a child, they should lay in bed in the Name of God, not filled with lust and passion. Although that is a part of the process of procreation, God must be in our consciousness when we are trying to conceive life. Women must desire to bring forth a child on this earth, male or female, who will make a difference in this world. They must think about it and pray for it.

When we say our prayers, we repeat the powerful attributes of Allah: *Bismillah ir-Rahman, ir-Rahim.* (In The Name of Allah, The Beneficent, The Merciful.) *Al-hamdu lilah rabbi al-amin.* (Praise be to Allah, The Lord, Nourisher, Sustainer, and Evolver of creation to its eventual perfection.) *Ir-Rahman, ir-Rahim.* (The Beneficent, The Merciful.) *Maaliki yawmid-deen.* (Master of the Day of Judgment.)

A woman should say to herself: "I want to produce a master. I want to produce one who masters the law, who is beneficent, who is merciful, and who will bow down to the God that will evolve him to perfection. I want my child to be guided on the right path. I want him guided to the path of the favor of God." She should keep repeating and thinking these thoughts until she starts fashioning a baby after the workings and attributes of God.

We should start talking to the baby once we know that life has been conceived. Do not wait until the child is born; start talking to the child while it is growing in the womb. Sound travels on water, and the baby grows in a bag of water in the womb. Ears develop that can hear, although eyes are not yet developed that can see. So, talk to the baby in the womb.

Recite the Holy Qur'an to the baby. Recite the Words of God to the baby. Recite your love for the child and your joy of having this new life and the opportunity to make a difference in the world. Keep repeating it. Do not let anything in your environment cause you to become negative, even if it is a negative circumstance. Exalt yourself over it with a positive attitude. Speak the Word of God so you can maintain a positive frame of mind so that the negativity of circumstances will not interfere with the positive nature of the Word of God.

As you develop life from conception in the womb to the minds of men and women, make them pregnant with the Word of Light. Talk to the child while it is in the womb. Teach it, read to it, but not silly fairy tales. Read to it the most beautiful narratives and stories. Read the most beautiful attributes into the child. Write on the paper of the mind of the child. Stamp his mind with your heartfelt desires for God and bring forth a child in the image and likeness of God.

Men should do this, too. A man should hold the hands of his pregnant wife and walk unashamed with her because she is in the most beautiful stage of her life. She is bringing forth new life that may save the world from its wretched self. As she loses the shape of her body, men should reform the shape of her mind. Make sure that all harmful influences are kept from her mind. Do not let her go to funerals because she should not be thinking about death while she is making life, even if it is the funeral of a dear one. It is better to remember the purpose of your life. Do not bring a pregnant woman around death and grieving people. This is what the Messenger, the Honorable Elijah Muhammad, taught.

Tell her that she should stay at home and think about the good things of the life that has passed away, rather than going where people are screaming, hollering, and falling out, trying to pacify themselves over their mistreatment of the one who is departed. Tell her you would like to take her to the movies, but it is unfit for her to see. Tell her that you want her to see good things so she can bring forth a good child. This is the second stage.

The third stage is the stage of nursing. Anyone who takes a baby from the breast of its mother is committing a crime against humanity because a cow cannot raise a human being. The White man has perfected the science of chemistry. He understands how to make a chemical pill that makes people happy, even though all the conditions around them are terribly sad. Then he has another pill that is a downer and another that will make you tell the truth, even if you want to lie. We need to know our brain is a chemical factory that works with the liver. If you want to be happy and you think the right kind of thoughts, you can produce the right chemistry that will lift your mood.

If you want to produce thoughts that will bring your mood down, if you keep thinking about negative things, eventually, you will get weak. Our mood shifts are caused by the chemical changes in our bodies from the thoughts that course through our brains.

In Lesson No. 2, Question #8, the Honorable Elijah Muhammad mentions water being drawn up from the earth's surface that gets into currents that are very swift and changeable. A cold current is swift and changeable. It can switch back and forth between cold and warmth. The mind is that way because the brain sits in water. When you put the wrong current on the brain, it can become frozen.

A person can be warm and loving one day, come in contact with someone very critical and negative, and then become frozen and cold. That person will begin saying "cold" words because the mind has become cold. But that mind can thaw out if that person is put in a warm current by getting around people with life in them.

So, a pregnant woman must have warm currents surrounding her brain. After a woman has a baby, men should not change the current around her. Her focus turns to watching out for the baby. Even though her husband may want to resume sexual relations with his wife, the baby comes first.

I was jealous of my first child, Betsy Jean, when my pretty wife would tend to her, and I wanted to talk to her. While she looked after the baby, I was a big baby lying beside her in the bed. As men, we have to grow up and recognize that a new life is here and that our babies need the attention of their mothers. We cannot get upset because our women are not able to pay us the same kind of attention as before. When fights break out, a woman still has to nurse the baby. When she is upset, the chemistry of her mind changes, affecting her blood and her milk. So, the baby is drinking the rejection of its father from the breasts of its upset mother.

Men must understand that women are co-operators with God. Women should not depend on formula or cow's milk to nurture their children. Many women believe that if they nurse, they will lose their forms, when in fact, women lose their forms when they do not nurse. They are destroying the value of their milk and hurting themselves because nature has a way, through the sucking process, of pulling the womb back into place. Nursing helps women heal after childbirth.

It is also a bonding period between the mother and her baby. The woman is healing on the inside, and the baby is being bonded to the mother through the milk in her breasts. If mothers continue to think good and right thoughts, the energy and chemistry of those thoughts transfer to their breast milk. Through nursing, mothers can reinforce what they wrote on the pages of the brains of their children while they were forming in the womb.

As mothers feed and develop their children, they must also foster an atmosphere of love. Then, you will have given birth to a giant that will make you like Mary. Every time we talk about Jesus, we talk about Mary; and every time the world talks about your children, they will talk about you because you will make yourself remembered by what you produce. Black woman, this is your day. This is your time. God is with you to bless your womb and fill you with His Spirit so that you will produce spirit-filled children of great vision. Women must prepare themselves.

Men should take another look at their women. Before men get into an argument and rock the jaws of their women, they should think about who rocks the cradle. It is better to walk away from the argument and cool down. Do not beat women because, if you do, God will make men feel the weight of punishment for interfering with the womb that is His co-operator in bringing forth new life.

II
PURIFICATION

8
Blessed is the Fruit of Thy Womb

Although the fourth Chapter of the Holy Qur'an is entitled "The Women," the 19th Chapter, entitled "Maryam," is the only chapter named after a specific woman, a woman with whom all Christians are familiar—Mary or, in Arabic, Maryam. Muslims, followers of the Teachings of the Holy Qur'an, have a disagreement with Christians regarding Mary. Some Christians have erroneously taken Jesus and his mother, Mary, as gods beside Allah, the Creator of the heavens and earth.

In the Bible, Jesus consistently talks about One greater than himself. He is very consistent in his devotion and love for the Father. If Jesus were the equal of God the Creator, he would not have to look to God for comfort, guidance, nurturing, etc. But Jesus says, "I can of myself do nothing." He is not an independent man. Jesus said that which the Father directs him to do, he does; and that which the Father tells him to speak, he speaks. Jesus is bearing witness that he is not the Originator of the Truth, but he is listening for God to speak to him, and he speaks to the people only what he hears from God. What God bids him to do is what he does. He is a perfect servant of Allah.

In the Book of John, Chapter 17:3, Jesus says: "And this is life eternal, that they might know Thee the only true God, and Jesus Christ, whom You have sent." He is talking about someone else: "the only true God and Jesus Christ, whom You have sent." The sender is greater than that which is sent. Jesus did not say, "I came into the world." He was sent into the world for us. He said: while I was with them in the world, I kept them in Thy Name—not in "my" name, but in "Your" Name, Father.

These scriptural passages plainly reject the false concept that Allah (God) has a partner or an associate. Jesus was not an associate of God or a partner of God. He was a servant of God. Therefore, when he was on the cross and felt forsaken, he cried out, "Father, My God, why has Thou forsaken me?" When he was ready to give up the ghost, he said, "Father, into Your Hands do I commend my spirit." He is talking about One greater than himself.

In the Holy Qur'an, Jesus says, "I said nothing to them except as You commanded me: to serve, to worship Allah, my Lord and your Lord." These words bear witness to scriptures in the Book of John. Jesus is not trying to get his followers to worship him. He is trying to get his followers to worship God perfectly. He said, "Worship God in spirit and in truth, for the Father seeketh such to worship Him." Jesus is talking about One greater than himself.

Muslims reject the elevation of Mary to such an exalted position as described in the "Hail Mary" prayer of the Catholic Church, which says: "Hail Mary, full of grace. The Lord is with Thee. Blessed art thou among women and blessed is the fruit of thy womb, Jesus. Hail Mary, Mother of God, pray for us sinners now and at the hour of our death. Amen." Mary can pray for you or me if she is around. You can pray for me, and I can pray for you. But God never made Mary an intercessor for people with Him. So, Muslims reject that part of Christian theology. Muslims must be careful in such rejection, lest in rejecting something, they do not see value in it and throw it away completely; and then take an extreme position to the negative, which hurts you.

Mary, the mother of Jesus, is a very special woman. No other woman, not even the mother of Prophet Muhammad, is mentioned in the Qur'an. If Prophet Muhammad (peace be upon him) is the greatest of all the prophets who ever lived, and the Seal of the prophets, his mother should be mentioned in the Book. But Mary is mentioned over her.

If a chapter of a book of eternal wisdom is devoted to a woman, then we need to pay attention to what Allah (God) is trying to teach us through the written Word and the revealed Word. There is something about that woman we need to study—not only the woman but what the woman produced.

On the other hand, Christians should not exalt Mary in a spooky way. Women should try to understand why Mary holds such a very high and special place in the scripture of both the Bible and Holy Qur'an. There was, in fact, a woman who existed called Mary. Chapter 19 of the Holy Qur'an is devoted to Mary. The number "19" appears in the 74th Surah or Chapter of the Holy Qur'an, where it is called the "Parable of 19."

A parable is a story that hides a deeper meaning than what the parable implies on the surface. In the number 19, there is a "1," which represents God, Who says He is One. And there is a "9," which represents the completion of the language of mathematics. When we put 1 and 9 together, we get 10, which represents all of the numbers of mathematics. With the entire language of mathematics, we can begin to build anything.

In the solar system, there are nine planets, and the 10th planet is the sun. The sun, in Arabic called *Al Shams*, is feminine and referred to as "she." If the sun is the giver of life, light, and energy and sits near the center and controls the movement of the spheres of life around her, then the Parable of 19, entitled "Maryam," contains a deep secret. When the secret is finally exposed, we will be able to see Allah (God). But you cannot see God except through her. The world of Islam needs a great reformation regarding the way men understand the woman. You can never be a great people or great nation or go where Allah (God) wants you to go if we disrespect the woman.

The 1 and 9 represent the universe. The universe you see came from a universe you did not see—meaning the universe that is seen springs forth from a womb that God, Himself, used His powers to produce out of the dark womb of space all that you see.

He said, "Be." Be what? Be a light. Then the sun comes forward. I want you to think about that. Before He said, "Be," it was there, but nobody could bring it forward. When the Power of God could command it, it had to come forth because a greater power was exercising itself on the womb to bring forth out of the womb its mysteries.

The universe is a pregnant universe that is constantly revealing new things. Allah (God) says in the Holy Qur'an that there are creatures you know and creatures of which you have no knowledge. The universe is such a mysterious womb that, whatever Allah (God) desires to bring forth, He brings it forth out of this magnificent womb. So, the universe is a pregnant universe because she is always coming up with new things.

9
The Womb is God's Laboratory

In the Holy Qur'an, Surah 4, verse 1, Allah (God) says He created man and his mate, or woman, of the same essence; and from these two, He spread many men and women. Then, Allah (God) orders us to reverence the womb.

Reverence carries a deep significance. To revere something is to hold it in awe and high esteem. The word "reverend" is the title given to one held in awe and high esteem because of spiritual gifts and wisdom. But truly, none is reverent but God.

Yet, Allah (God) says, "Reverence the womb." Why should we hold the womb in awe? We should reverence the womb because everything we see came forth out of this great, dark, mysterious, and magnificent womb by the Command of God Who acted upon that womb. Every one of us came forth out of that dark, mysterious chamber. Allah (God) commands us to reverence the

36

womb because we do not understand the power that is within it. The womb is God's laboratory.

The Honorable Elijah Muhammad taught us about the making of the White man. Although many Muslims reject this, Master Fard Muhammad, Who taught the Honorable Elijah Muhammad, knows what the scholars have yet to discover. If we truly reverenced the womb, we would not be surprised at what the womb could produce. Because we do not pay proper respect to the womb of a woman, we do not really understand the value of the woman and why a woman must never be abused or misused.

Women must begin to learn who they are, not from the scholars of the world, but from Allah (God), Who fashioned the woman after the womb of the universe from which He created everything. Men cannot advance except through the wombs of women. There cannot be any advancement for the world, society, or civilization except that it comes through the womb.

10
Environment Goes into the Nature of a Forming Life

Gregor Mendel, a White monk, discovered a law of pairs in genetics. According to Mendel's Law, light skin is recessive and dark skin is dominant. Light eyes are recessive and dark eyes are dominant. Recessive means weak, while dominant means strong. He discovered that the weaker could come from the stronger, but the process could not be reversed.

White anthropologists, White historians, White biologists, and White geneticists never argued with the Honorable Elijah Muhammad about the making of the White man. The deeper significance of that part of the Teachings of the Honorable Elijah Muhammad lies in understanding that the environment becomes incorporated into the nature of any life while it is forming. According to the Teachings of the Honorable Elijah Muhammad, lying and murder surrounded the making of White people on the island of Pelan. If lying and murder occur while life is being fashioned, then lying and murder become a part of the nature of that life.

The White man himself has not known why he lies as he does or why he is a murderer and blood-shedder of all the peoples of the earth. In Chapter 8 of the Book of John in the Bible, Jesus said, *"I know you. You are of your Father, the devil. The lust of your Father you shall do. He was a liar from the beginning and a murderer."* If the father was a liar and murderer, his offspring is what the father made.

This does not mean that we cannot overcome the tendency of nature, but the Caucasian has a natural tendency toward lying and murder. Because he is such a liar and murderer, he has actually spread his power over the womb of the Black woman, and they are producing liars and murderers from their wombs. Mothers are frightened of their own children, wondering from where they came. They came from you.

Women who complain that there are not enough good men in the world should understand that what we see in men is what women have produced. Women are actually condemning the fruit of their wombs. If something is wrong with the man, something is wrong with the woman. Unless what is wrong with women is fixed, there will never be better men for women to fall in love with-- because where there are no decent women, there are no decent men, for the woman is the Mother of Civilization. Women must take that responsibility.

In the Book of Proverbs in the Bible, it reads, "A wise child maketh a glad father, but a foolish child is the heaviness of its mother." Women can make their children foolish or wise. Women can make their children devils or gods. Through their wombs, women possess the power to fashion life. But women must decide what kind of children they desire to produce.

The first work of the Honorable Elijah Muhammad was to try his very best to reform the Black woman because, unless a genuine reformation occurs with the Black woman, Black people do not have any future at all. That is the importance of the woman. Whenever a strong Black man emerges among our people— understanding the value of the Black woman, reverencing the womb, and doing that which is his duty by the Black woman—the White man will lie, scheme, and destroy him because the White man has his hand over the womb of the Black woman. His hand is the hand of death. So, out of the wombs of Black women, death and destruction are coming to our people and society.

Children today are like grapes of wrath. They will set your teeth on edge. They do not have any natural love for their parents and will sometimes kill their parents when their parents try to reprimand them. Although the Holy Qur'an teaches that children should honor and respect their mother and father, children today will not only disrespect their parents, but they will also curse, beat, and kill their parents. Today, children will lock their parents up at an old age and take their money.

This is what the wombs of women have produced. Women cannot blame it on school or society alone because women have made society. All of it came from the wombs of women.

11
Children Born from Lust

Most children are born out of total lust. Men meet women at parties after they have been smoking or drinking. Women dress in tight clothing to be seductive to a man while she walks or dances. These low-down circumstances program the mind on a low level.

The Bible says how people would heap to themselves teachers that would tickle their ears. The ear is a very sensitive thing. A woman does not usually go after the ear of a man. It is usually a man who goes after the ear of a woman. The ear is the organ that leads to submission. So, when a man is dancing with a woman, he is tickling her ear with words. From the ear to the neck runs the jugular vein. In the Holy Qur'an, Allah (God) says He is closer to us than our life vein.

When a man drops from the ear to the neck, he is coming in the path of God to bring a woman under subjection to his will. The woman does not object because she came to the party to come under subjection. Instead of fighting the feeling, the woman encourages the feeling. So, the man and woman become two animals, breathing hard.

Nature and life are beautiful and wonderful. In one form or another, we have all experienced this feeling. We yield under that passion because Allah (God) gives us passion. He gives us the ability to love. But when love is not cultivated or developed, a fleshy lust exists that culminates in a sexual relationship.

When a woman finds herself pregnant for a man she may know very little about, he does not feel the need to commit to her. He may disappear from the woman's life, but that does not change the fact that she has a life growing inside her that she may no longer want.

Very few of us were produced through the planning of our parents. We were accidentally conceived during a lustful evening. The thought that empowered and generated the sperm originated from a low mind because it was based on lust. The beginning of the child forms on that same lustful principle. It is incredibly sad that we do not reverence that womb.

Because the White man is frightened by the power of the womb of the Black woman, he makes it easy to have an abortion. If a woman has had abortions, it is not my intention to make her feel guilty. If she is plagued by guilt, God wants her to feel guilty. But there is a way out of this situation.

God is not going to beat her up or kill her because of the silliness she does in ignorance. When we know better, we must do better. The White man and our own weaknesses make us parties to murder. We contribute to murder every time we engage in sex—which is an act of a responsible man and woman—but we want pleasure and not responsibility.

The man and woman conspire to murder and try all kinds of things to get rid of the life forming inside her. That spirit of murder is pervasive now. When the child is finally born, because the woman may have been afraid to have an abortion or tried to kill it and eventually changed her mind, the baby comes here unloved from the womb.

The mother did not love the child in the womb because she did not want it. She did not nurture it in the womb. Instead, she was partying, smoking, drinking, snorting, or putting crack in her veins. She was killing the fruit of her womb from the very beginning. The Black woman is killing herself because she does not know who she is. Black women do not reverence their wombs because they do not know the power of God in the womb. Instead of dwelling on the pain of an abortion, a woman should dwell on the hope of what tomorrow will bring when her mind, body, and whole being get right.

Because lying and murder are the order of the day, children are birthed into that kind of environment. Today, children kill at younger ages and have become the most violent because they were birthed into a world that did not want them from the beginning. Suicide is one of the main killers of young people because mothers tried to get rid of them before they were even born. It is mothers who have produced these children from their thinking.

12
Training under a New Light of Civilization

The world has produced Hitler, Attila, Genghis Khan, Tamerlane, and Napoleon—people who have killed by the tens of thousands. The world has also produced Abraham, Moses, and Jesus. All of these men came from the womb of a woman.

Mary was a special woman. Mary grew up in the temple under the Law of Moses. It was a strict law. One did not commit adultery. One did not commit fornication. One did not steal. One did not bear false witness against thy neighbor. One did not covet the possessions of thy neighbor. One honored thy mother and father. One did not set up and worship any god but the One God. One did not make any image. Moses taught Israel the proper foods to eat.

When a woman is raised under that kind of law and eats divinely prescribed foods, her body is clean. Mary meditated on God and glorified God in her thoughts. As a child, she was told that she would bring forth an anointed child, so he was a desire in her. We cannot have anything but what we desire or strive. When most women conceive life, their only desire is for fleshly sexual fulfillment. They do not think, "I want to produce into the world someone to change this condition." But when women come under a law and teaching as Moses brought, she does.

The Holy Qur'an says Allah (God) would give us a man like Moses. We cannot have a man like Moses, except we have a condition like the Children of Israel suffering under Pharaoh. Black people have been in America for over 400 years under the White man and needed someone to bring us a strong law, like Moses. The Honorable Elijah Muhammad gave us that kind of law. Every woman who became a part of the Honorable Elijah Muhammad's reform came under that strict law.

The Honorable Elijah Muhammad improved on it and taught us how to eat to live. He named the women's class "Muslim Girls in Training and General Civilization Class" or M.G.T.-G.C.C. because women were not grown up in the way of God. They were girls in the Way of God and received training, under the guiding light of a Man of God, into a new way of civilization. That training dealt with cooking, sewing, cleaning your house, how to care for your husband, how to rear your children, and how to act at home and abroad. He brought a new knowledge, a new wisdom, and a new understanding. With it, Elijah Muhammad reformed the complete minds of Black women. He was making Maryam.

Maryam of the 19th Surah of the Holy Qur'an is the ideal woman from whose womb will come messianic saviors of the world. It is a picture of the Black woman, the "n-----r" woman, the woman who has been spat on, cursed, abused, and misused. Allah (God) has chosen the Black woman to bring forth saviors for the entire world. But the Black woman must make a change in her life.

The Christian prayer says, "Holy Mary, Mother of God," not mother of Allah because Allah is not begotten, nor does He beget. But women can birth a mental giant, a god with force and power. Women can bring into the world one who can master the forces of nature. Women can bring into the world one who can stand above all men, like the top of Mount Everest, and we do not have to wait 100 generations to do it.

Regardless of age, if a woman has an egg that is alive, she can do it. But women must stop negative behaviors, and men must help them stop. However, if a man does not know what to do with a woman, he should leave her alone. If a man does not know what to do with himself, he should stop his negative behaviors. We have been abusing ourselves for too long. Some guests checked their cigarettes at the security post before they entered this meeting. Doctors are filling us up with numerous medicines and pills for various illnesses. All these chemicals are breaking down our bodies. These chemicals are becoming a part of the egg that is the future of new life. We must clean up our bodies. Women cannot make a Jesus, a world savior, with a contaminated womb and a mind that does not love God but hates self and rejects responsibility.

As long as we are content in glorifying what Mary did in the past, we cannot accept that we have work to do today. Women are content with finger-popping, partying, opening their legs to any man who comes along, and producing evil fruit from their wombs. This is unacceptable. We must do it right this time.

Women can change the world with their wombs, but a new thought must take root in their minds. Not a thought to simply lie down with a man, but a thought to lie down and bring God forth from the womb. That is why Jesus said we must love God with all our hearts, all of our souls, and all of our minds. If women love God this way, they will look for a man who loves God that way. When she sees him, he will be like any other man, only the Spirit of God will be all in him.

Women can save the world. Women all over the world need to know who they are because, if they knew, they would take care of themselves. Even if a man was not who he should be to a woman, she could take his sperm and make something out of it if she knew what to do with herself. We have an overwhelming number of wicked men all over the earth, but we do not have any righteous men or men of giant thinking and strong character who will stand up against this wicked enemy and put him down. It begins with the woman.

The Honorable Elijah Muhammad said 75 percent of his work is with the women. Men are 25 percent of the problem, while women are almost the whole problem. If we get the woman right, we will have a future. Men do not know what to do with women. When men try to teach women by instructing women to listen only to them, men are not successful in cultivating women. It would be better for men to let a Friend help them learn how to relate to women. Since God created the woman, He is the Best Knower of how to cultivate her.

Men should not feel as if they are being neglected in this matter. If the woman is 75 percent of the problem and 75 percent of the work, and the earth consists of three-quarters water and one-quarter land, and all living things originate from water, then the woman is the source of new life.

So, men should not mistreat women. A man should not beat a woman, even if she makes him angry. It is better for the man to walk out. Do not beat women. This is a terrible thing for a man to do, even though some women beat men today. There is much hatred between the Black male and the Black female. We cannot produce good children out of this hatred.

13
We Must Clean Up Our Bodies

Women should think about themselves and begin cleaning up their bodies. Smoking hurts your health. When we absorb such poisons into our blood, that blood forms the brain of a baby. We do not want to destroy a baby's chance to become a visionary. That is why we must clean up our lives. We do not need to drink. We do not need to use drugs. We need to begin thinking now about what we would like to produce from the womb.

If Jesus was the desire of all women, then women must become conscious of the kind of child they could produce from their wombs in order for him to be a desire. It is not that women would desire Jesus the prophet of 2,000 years ago; they would desire to produce a messianic figure today.

When we look at the condition of the world and the condition of our people, we must wonder how we can solve the condition. Women must produce children from their wombs to make a change in the world. It does not make a difference if the child is male or female because women can also change the condition of the world.

First, women must prepare and clean up their bodies. Men must also clean up their bodies because sperm represents the future of life and is sacred. Men poison their sperm every time they consume alcohol, smoke cigarettes, or take drugs. These poisons are reflected in a man's sperm and can be seen in a sample of a man's urine. If poisons are in the urinary tract, they get into the blood. If poisons are in the blood, they get into the sperm.

Men are killing our future and must clean up. Men must come under the Divine Law of God, begin thinking on a higher level, and desire to produce a child who will help turn this world around. We must understand that only the womb of the woman is going to produce such a child.

I am simply your Brother, a human being—but an angel is only one who bears a message. So, like Mary, an angel of the Lord has come to you to give you good news that God desires to give you a pure child. Even if a woman doubts that she can produce a pure child because she is barren, too old, or has not produced a good child in the past, I am a bearer of the good news that God desires to give her a pure child.

Women must clean up and prepare their bodies to receive the child. If a man has prepared himself and the woman has prepared herself, they should plan to conceive life together. They should learn to identify the fertile days of the woman. We usually find out for evil purposes. So why not find out for a good purpose?

Women should not get pregnant right away. They should take some time to get their bodies cleaned up and their minds in better shape. They should begin to desire to produce the kind of child who will change the condition of our people and the world. Women must determine in their minds, "I want to produce a child who will help alleviate the conditions of sickness, disease, ignorance, and death." Women must recognize their importance by understanding that they are co-operators and co-creators with God. They must realize that their actions and behaviors at the time of conception are central to the quality of the child that they will form and produce from their wombs.

14
How to Restore a Woman's Natural Love

The Bible says, "God is love." The creative force behind all creation is love. We possess the power to love. When a woman does not have any love for the life forming within her, she cannot produce a child in the image and likeness of God. So, it behooves a man to work the field of a woman's mind to cultivate her natural ability to love. A man should not plant his seed within a woman before he cultivates her natural ability to love.

The worst thing a man can do is try to find his way to the secret parts of a woman before he finds a way to cultivate her natural love for him. Sex is not first; it is last. It is the culmination of a developing love. It is not a base expression. It is the highest expression of two people who genuinely love one another. When a woman "falls in love," it changes her almost instantly. People will look at her and say, "You look different." Most women have loved like this once in their life, but hardly ever again. After a woman loves like that and suffers hurt—which all women have been—she never returns to the quality of that first love again unless God Himself restores her natural love.

This natural love is part of the innocence of girls, which is at the root of why some fathers fall in love with their young daughters and tamper with them. I did not understand the dynamic of sexual abuse at first, but I began to study it. When a wife grows away from her husband, she no longer desires to cater to him. If her young daughter loves her father, the daughter will want to cater to her father when her mother is too tired. The daughter will fix meals and do other things to serve her father.

The daughter looks like the mother used to look before the mother became tired of caring for herself and turned overweight, out of shape, ugly, and ugly-acting. The husband becomes dissatisfied with his wife, while the daughter loves her father with a pure love. Most men have never seen such a love in his wife because most women lost that pure love long before they got married, either when they first lost their virtue or when a previous man hurt them.

Women should not become angry with this reality. Most men never experience the true beauty and innocence of a woman because once a woman gets hurt, she withdraws herself. The pain is so great that she thinks she will die, so she never wants to experience that pain ever again.

Men have experienced the same kind of pain after a man loves intensely once and gets hurt—probably because he met a woman after another man hurt her. When he tells a woman he loves her, she looks at him with disbelief, recalling the painful past of an unloving man. She makes the new man suffer. At the end of the relationship, the man determines to take advantage of every woman who will come into his life. And so does the woman. With such a mentality, men and women use each other. We never love each other. Sex becomes a weapon and tool to gain leverage to get money from each other.

Mothers must learn how to protect their homes and how to protect themselves. After women have children, they should never stop taking care of themselves—their health, beauty, and weight. Even if a woman does not have a man who loves her, she should love herself enough to care for herself. A woman should put the best food in her body. She should eat fresh fruit and vegetables, not canned or frozen food. She should eat food while life is in it, as well as learn how to properly cook food so that she does not cook the life out of it. When a woman feeds herself, she will then feed life into her body. A woman will make tissues, flesh, nerves, and nearly six miles of veins out of the food she eats. She will be fashioning the brain of her child out of the food she eats.

A man can make a woman love again. It will be difficult in the beginning, but a man must be persistent and consistently good to a woman. She will not be able to help herself when she meets the Spirit of God in a well-made man. Regardless of how cold-hearted a woman has become, she will soften her heart for a man if he comes to her with the Spirit of God. A man cannot restore a woman's natural, pure love without submission and obedience to Allah (God).

Even though it is beneficial for a man to have a wonderful and strong body, it is better for a man to have a strong character and a strong will to achieve. It is better for a man to be a loving human being. Women love men who are loving. A man must be wise in order to restore a woman's natural love.

15
Natural Love is the Power of the Womb

Natural love in a woman lights up her being because the essence of her creation is love. That is the power of her womb. It is love. When a man can restore that natural spark in a woman, she wants to have a baby for him. She will not run from pregnancy and chase material things.

Even though a woman will talk about seeking material things before pregnancy, the real issue is that she does not want to have a baby for the man she is with because he has not awakened that natural love in her. When a man wakes up the natural love in a woman for him, she wants to produce that man again. When a woman loves a man, the greatest thing she can do is to have that man growing inside her. When she loves a man, she desires to do that for him. And she is truly doing something for him, for her people, and, above all, for God.

After a woman learns of her pregnancy, her attention strays a bit from the father. The man may feel that something is wrong because she may become a little cold to him. But she is focusing on the life growing within her. She needs to focus all her love on that forming life in her womb from the first day that she learns that she is pregnant. She should begin to think about what she desires to do for God with that child.

The stronger she desires to give birth to a child who will be a blessing to the world, she will begin to write the future as she forms the mind of the new life. The child is already born with certain gifts and talents, but the mother will actually help form that mind, that leaning, and that spirit. The woman and God.

That is why a woman must pray. A woman who prays is pouring her earnest desires out to God, and her prayers impress upon the womb. When a woman is pregnant, she should stop going to the movies because this world's films are filled with cursing, violence, and killing. A man should keep a woman away from such negative influences because she is making a child to bring an end to the negativity in the world.

The man should stay with his woman because she will be inclined to think that he is rejecting her because her shape is changing. Instead of running out of the house to hang out with his friends, he needs to stay with her when she is pregnant.

As her stomach grows bigger, the man should oil it so that she does not get stretch marks. As the man oils her stomach and massages it gently, he should talk to the new life forming in the womb. The fetus is floating in a bag of water while it is forming, and the water will transmit sound. The fetus has ears. So, pick up your Holy Qur'an and read to the baby.

The first command that Allah (God) gave to Prophet Muhammad was "Read, in the Name of your Lord," which is found in the Chapter entitled "The Clot." While your baby is a clot, you should read in the Name of your Lord. Read to your baby while it is forming in the womb. Read in the Name of your Lord, Who taught man by the pen what man knew not. You should talk to your child while it is forming in the womb and tell the child what you want it to be and do in its life.

A man must work with the pregnant woman every day. He should work with her stomach, work with her mind, and work with her diet because she is working for God. She is producing a child to turn around this crazy world. As the baby begins to kick and move, the man should be present with the woman to enjoy every moment. God is present with the new life inside the darkness of the womb.

Even though the father and mother are on the outside, the woman is actually also on the inside because her thoughts are going into the womb. That is why the man must keep the pregnant woman happy. As the saying goes, "She's got one in the oven" — you do not stomp around the oven while a cake is baking. So, a man should not do crazy things with a woman while she is carrying his life inside her womb.

A man should give her good things to feed her mind. Women should not watch soap operas and, in fact, should turn off the television. She should feed on good news so she can focus on producing a pure child. She should not focus on the sex of the child but rather on the purity of the child. This is what we call an "immaculate conception." As time goes on and you continue to read to the child the Words of Allah, talk to the child. You're constantly talking to it, from within.

Every day and night, the man and woman should talk to the baby and shower love on it. Men should also shower love on the woman. If there are other children in the house, the entire family should shower love on the expecting mother and the child in the womb so that the other children will anxiously want the new child to come into the world. This will create a whole environment of love. God is love.

If a woman wants to produce a devil and destroyer from her womb, she can do it. If a woman wants to produce a savior from her womb, she can do it. It all depends on the woman.

.

III
REFORMATION

16

The Oppression of Women Must End

All over the earth, women are rising to speak up and speak out against injustice. This is the day when the oppressed of the earth will speak out against their oppressors. If we are oppressed in America, it is nothing but right and just that we speak out against oppression. As we speak out against our oppression, our Brothers and Sisters in Africa, the Caribbean, and throughout the world speak out against their oppression, and persons of varying races and colors speak out against their oppression, we notice women all over the world are speaking out against, not perceived oppression but very real and tangible oppression.

In the United States, one of the most advanced societies presently on the earth, women are considered playthings. In a so-called advanced society, women are considered playthings. So how advanced can that society be? In Europe, women are also considered playthings. In many parts of the Islamic world, although Muslims pay lip service to the great liberation effort of Prophet Muhammad (peace be upon him), women are relegated to lesser roles in society or no role in society at all. Women are relegated to a less-than-human position in many Islamic states.

In many cultures, women are definitely oppressed. So how advanced can this world be if the leaders of the world have denigrated the position of women? If so-called primitive societies have not elevated the woman, then the nations of the world are depressed, oppressed, and suppressed. The greatest oppression and suppression are fomented by ignorance.

The Honorable Elijah Muhammad—a man born among us, a man whom we believe is the Messenger of God, a man who worked to reform us for 44 years while he was among us—taught that "No nation can rise any higher than its women." If a nation wants advancement, it must exalt the woman. If a nation wants to ascend to the heights that Allah (God) intends for it to rise, it must exalt the woman. Exaltation does not mean putting women on a pedestal or, as in some primitive societies, worshipping the woman. The exaltation of women actually means allowing them to be what Allah (God) has created them to be.

The Holy Qur'an teaches us to "reverence the womb that bore you." If we reverence the womb, we should develop a feeling or attitude of deep respect, love, and awe for something sacred. The womb of a woman is sacred. The womb of a woman should awe not only women but also men. A minuscule drop of sperm can be deposited in the darkness of a womb, and when that uterus closes around this speck of sperm, something wonderful takes place. That is something that we should hold in awe because we did not have any hand in the process, but a Mighty Hand is working in the womb.

Children should hold in deep respect, love, and awe their mothers. Every female child should hold in deep awe and respect her own person, for she is blessed with this masterful, mysterious source of goodness called the womb. Girls, young women, middle-aged women, and older women should all have a deep respect for themselves and awe for the position in which Allah (God) has placed them.

Females should know from a young age that they are blessed with a womb, and because of their wombs, they are co-operators and co-creators with God. Women are blessed with the womb of the future. If women are suppressed, if women are oppressed, if women are considered objects of pleasure to be used, abused, and discarded, then as a people, we can never rise because we do not have any reverence for the womb.

17
Society Should Free Women

In His Infinite Mercy and Power, Allah (God) has set the earth on flame with two great powerful forces that the Holy Qur'an calls Gog and Magog or Juj and Majuj. According to the scholars, Gog and Magog will surge against each other, and then the trumpet will be blown. The Holy Qur'an says, "We will gather them all together." Another part of the Holy Qur'an says that Gog and Magog are let loose, and they will sally forth from every exalted place or every point of eminence.

According to the Teachings of the Holy Qur'an, Allah (God) says, *"I have created some of my servants whom no one can destroy but Myself."* Allah says that Gog and Magog are such powerful forces that when they are let loose in the earth, it will create upheaval. Nation will rise against nation and kingdom against kingdom; then will the Kingdom of Heaven come, the Kingdom that all the prophets heralded. The Kingdom of heaven comes on the heels of a great battle between Gog and Magog.

The scholars say that Gog and Magog are the Teutonic and Slavic peoples of the earth. The European powers have emerged as the great powers of the earth, and they have sallied forth. A wall built to hold the Europeans in Europe tumbled down, and they sallied forth—going west, east, north, and south, seeking whom they might devour. In the conflict of these European powers over the spoils of the world, the darker people of the earth have become the victims of Gog and Magog, or the Teutonic and Slavic races of the world, the Europeans and Caucasians.

Out of this has come democracy and capitalism, which claim to exalt the right of the individual. In reality, these systems exalt a few individuals that they might enslave the masses of individuals to work for little or nothing for the benefit of the few whose greed and lust for the material goods of the world have exceeded the limits. The Europeans who came westward into Western Europe and America lift God with their mouths, but their hearts are far removed from the practice of godliness or righteousness.

They promote Jesus as a Caucasian to the darker peoples with the mind to get the Black, Brown, and Yellow peoples to worship the Caucasian image. It is a sin to promote a color of Jesus and hide his goodness and message so that the darker peoples receive a watered-down concoction of Europeans, who mixed truth with falsehood. They hid the truth while they knew and put Jesus' name on what they concocted.

This, Muhammad called a dirty religion; not that the name "Jesus" is dirty or that his teachings are dirty, but the practice of so-called Christians is a dirty practice. To kill off the Indigenous peoples, enslave Black people, and rob us of the knowledge of self is a dirty practice. To go into Mexico and Central America and take their land and leave them in poverty and want is a dirty religion. Jesus was clean, but the practice of so-called Christians in his name is a dirty practice.

In this dirty practice, though they claim to exalt Mary, the mother of Jesus, they actually make a mockery of Mary and womanhood by cheapening women, regardless of their color. They design immodest clothes for women, create dances that a dog would be ashamed to dance, and elicit lust in the hearts of women and men so that the private parts of women and men are absolutely worshipped. So, women are degraded, used, and abused in so-called Christendom.

On the other side of the world, the other part of the European, Teutonic, and Slavic people developed communism, which is a denial of God. Yet, it is a progression. The Honorable Elijah Muhammad said when Gog and Magog are let loose and sally forth from every exalted place means that, worldwide, communism would start striking from every exalted place and challenging the greed of capitalism, the suppression, oppression, and abuse of the working force, and the oppression of women.

Everywhere in the world that I have traveled to a socialist country, I have seen women freer and taking part in building that society. They do not talk so much about God. They talk about the exaltation of the man and the woman, which is a step in the right direction. Communism has taken hold in China, where they allow people to practice religion, but they cannot proselytize religion because they say religion is the opiate of the people, according to Marxist/Leninist philosophy. And they are not wrong.

Religion has been used to drug people into believing intolerable conditions are more acceptable. Religion and singing hymns are used to lull people to sleep to the reality of the fact that they are not getting true religion. The people are getting a made-up concoction attached to the holy name of Jesus that does not have any power to bring them out of their condition.

Godless communism is challenging godless democracy and godless hypocrisy. The greed of materialism from the East is challenging the greed of materialism in the West. This constant battle today between communism and capitalism is giving rise to a third force in the world—the sleeping Nation of Islam, which not only refers to the Lost and Found members of that great Aboriginal nation in the West.

The Nation of Islam consists of over one billion Muslims on this earth who are asleep today under the rubbish of Arab nationalism, their own nationalism, and the domination of spook-ism and unreality.

With the sallying forth of Gog and Magog, this third force is arising in the world. The third force is Islam, the true religion of Allah, the religion of entire obedience and submission to His Will. Islam is that great religious force today that is rising to give balance to these two materialist forces—godless communism and godless capitalism under the hypocrisy of religion.

18
The Kingdom of God Must Be on Earth

Islam is rising in the world. But in its rise, it has to pull the cover off itself. Islam has to purify and cleanse itself to prepare to bring in the Kingdom of God. It has to be reformed and revived. In the Islamic world, the desire to return religion to its fundamental purity has produced clashes between Muslims. There is a desire to cleanse it from the Marxist/Leninist doctrine that has crept into some Islamic, socialist thought. There is a desire to cleanse it from the Western imperialist thought that has crept into Islam. So, the world of Islam is in convulsion. But all things work for good for those who love the Lord.

Those pilgrims who were slaughtered in Mecca died not in vain, but their deaths were part of the revolution and evolution toward the ultimate Kingdom of God. "Thy Kingdom come on earth"—not in the sky. If the Kingdom of God is coming to the earth, what place will world leaders and governments have in it? These governments are to be removed, and a new kind of government set up: A government that is truly of the people, by the people, and for the people, a government based on the Law and Commandments of God.

Gog and Magog are let loose. The fighting is raging in every quarter of the globe. The oppressed are crying out for liberation. Godless communism aims to inspire revolution from the worker and the oppressed class. Those who love Marxist/Leninist thought are busy stirring up the masses to revolt against terrible conditions all over the world. In the wake of that stirring up, women are being stirred up. Women are emerging in socialist societies, showing their power, prowess, and intellectual capabilities. This challenges religious societies to answer the questions: "What have you done *to* your woman? What have you done *with* your woman?"

When you have something sacred, you put it in a sacred place. There is no loving Jew, Christian, or Muslim who will leave a symbol or relic of their religion in an unclean or un-reverential place. When Allah (God) says the woman should be in the home, He is not saying that a woman should not move abroad. But if abroad is contaminated, keep the woman at home where she can be protected because women are sacred and deserve to be in a sacred place.

Men who understand God, love God, and know the workings of God will kill nations to protect the wombs of their women. However, men are so hateful and disrespectful of themselves that they allow the wombs of their women to be contaminated with the filth and debris of every nation and people. I thank the Honorable Elijah Muhammad for teaching us that where there are no decent women, there are no decent men, for the woman is the Mother of Civilization.

How can we claim to worship Allah and then turn around and degrade women? If a man truly loves Allah, he will exalt his woman and protect her womb. He will put her in a sacred place like a sacred vessel and will not allow anyone to defile her vessel with wine, strong drink, or disease. This must be the mindset of a man. This is the duty of men of every nation on earth.

If we are going to make a change on the earth and the Kingdom of God is going to come to the earth, it will be birthed through a woman. This is why Mary is exalted. She is not exalted because God wants us to worship her. She is exalted because it is only when the woman is exalted that we can bring the Kingdom of God on earth.

The Honorable Elijah Muhammad said communism would be the steppingstone to the Kingdom of God, the Kingdom of Islam. Communism and capitalism are fighting against the rise of Islam. Former president Richard Nixon said that the real threat to democracy is not communism; it is fundamentalist Islam. What is Islam? It is obedience to the Will of God. Why do they seek to put a cover over Minister Farrakhan? They do not want us to be attracted to the majestic power of Islam.

19

A Change Needed

Islam was the religion of Jesus, the religion of the prophets, and the religion of God when He originated the heavens and the earth. Islam is not a new religion. It is as old as God Himself. Obedience to God's Will is the way He created the heavens and the earth. He created the sun and said, "Obey." He created the moon and said, "Obey." He created man and said, "Obey, if it pleases you." He gave the human being the free will to reject or accept God's Will. If we reject, we reject to our detriment. If we accept, we accept for our betterment.

We do not add to Allah, nor can we take away from Him. He is Allah, Self-Glorified. The heavens and the earth glorify Him. He does not need our praise. He is worthy of praise, even if we never praise Him. Everything in creation bears witness to His Majesty. We even bear witness in our rebellion.

In 1977, I visited Cuba and then traveled to the island of Barbados. When I arrived in Barbados, they had a press conference at the airport. The reporters asked, "How could you, a religious man, have visited godless Cuba?" and "What is your purpose in Barbados?" I recounted to them the parable of Jesus about two sons who were asked to do the will of the father. One said he would and did not; the other said he would not but did. Which one did the will of the father—the one who said it and did it not or the one who denied that he would but yet did it?

I reminded them that when western powers were in control in Cuba, the Cuban people were 90 percent illiterate, but today they have erased illiteracy. In Cuba, people do not have to have money to be healed if they become sick. They can go to the hospital for free health care. Education is free. Women are exalted and respected. America claims to love God and Jesus, but Jesus said, "Feed the hungry. Clothe the naked. Shelter the homeless. Visit the sick and the imprisoned. And if you have not done it unto the least of these, my brethren, you have not done it also unto me."

I told them that the poor in Barbados must have money to have an operation or go to college. Although Cuba is a communist country and therefore does not claim to follow God—or said it would not do the Will of the Father—evidently, the Will of the Father is being done in Cuba. America is a Judeo-Christian country and therefore claims to follow God—or said it would do the Will of the Father—but America has not done it. Capitalism and its greed and godless materialism must give way to the proper worship of God and a change on the earth. That change cannot come except a change is made in the status of women.

20
The Mind is a Womb

We must focus on changing the status of women. Men hurt their advancement when they abuse or mistreat women, use them for pleasure, and cast them aside as though they do not have any value. Women must understand that God did not create the female to be a vessel of pleasure. He created women after the universe. God used the dark womb of space as His laboratory and said, "Cum fia cum!" (Be and it is!). He brought all creation out of the dark womb of space as a sign to women blessed with a womb.

Women are blessed with a physical womb and also blessed with a mind that is another womb. As we reverence the womb with deep awe, love, and respect because it is sacred, we should also reverence the mind, for it is the laboratory of the working of a Mighty Creator. Whatever the mind can conceive and we can believe, we can achieve and bring it out of the thought stage into reality. As long as the mind is free to think on the unlimited wisdom of a Mighty and Infinite Creator, man will continue to build worlds and civilizations beyond our wildest imagination.

All day and all night, we are feeding our minds with filthy songs and television programs. It is no wonder America is on her way down to the depths of hell and destruction. There is no reverence for the womb of the woman and there is no reverence for the mind. A woman's brain is connected to her womb so that when she begins to fashion life in her physical womb, she is fashioning that life from the contents of her mind, her first womb.

Desire feeds the will. Human beings are gifted with a will like the Creator. We can say "Be" and bring into existence what we will. No other creature can do this but man and his Creator. With this ability, man and woman are above all creation. Therefore, all creation serves humanity.

If women do not have proper desires to feed their wills, what then can they produce from their physical wombs? Women must consider the circumstances that led to their pregnancy. They must consider the thoughts that were in their minds. Did they go to a party, see a handsome man and say, "I want him." So, a woman met the man of her choice, which must not have been too good: It is evident if she is alone now.

A poor decision took her in the wrong direction. As a result, she became a mother. The woman may have been feeling lonely. The man may have been looking and smelling good. The woman may have barely known the man's name when she conceived. So, neither the man nor the woman desired the child and may have considered abortion. When a child is aborted, a sacred womb has been violated and a sacred life is being murdered.

Because women do not have anything of value in their minds, they are not producing children of consequence. Children are a pain to their mothers because they are destroyed women. None of our teachers or leaders lifted our women until the Honorable Elijah Muhammad—who was taught by Master Fard Muhammad, to Whom praise is due forever—lifted them.

On the last day that the Honorable Elijah Muhammad delivered a major speech, he said the world was not doing anything with the woman and pointed to the Muslim women of the Nation of Islam in the audience. It was a sea of women who once wore miniskirts that were so tight that a sneeze would make them naked. They once had painted faces, going into many obscene places, fraternizing with the filth of many races, bringing upon us many, many disgraces. The Honorable Elijah Muhammad called the woman out of her filthy ways and put her in a new garment. He did not stop there. Many women wear long dresses. It just takes them a little longer to pull them up.

A long dress is not a key to heaven; it is only one of them. The Honorable Elijah Muhammad also called the woman to put a new thought in her mind because women must take charge of both of their wombs. They must know that they are co-operators with God in the creation of human life. If women have a strong enough desire, that desire will feed their wills, which will operate on their wombs, and they will produce the children they desire. But when women kill their minds, they kill desire.

By destroying a woman's knowledge of self, she does not know who she is and her purpose in the world, so she does not know what to desire. We must change the world. We cannot change the world unless we change and reform the thinking of women.

21
A Vow to God

The third Chapter of the Holy Qur'an is entitled "The Family of Amran." It mentions a woman of that family. You cannot create a family without a woman. The kind of family that you create is based upon the kind of woman that you have. It reads that a woman of Amran said, "My Lord, I vow to Thee what is in my womb to be devoted to Thy service, so accept it from me. Surely Thou, only Thou, art the Hearing and the Knowing." This is a woman of God. A woman must be God-conscious for her to do what God wants her to do: to co-operate with Him. She must know God. She must love God. God must be uppermost in her mind, not her husband or boyfriend.

No husband can do for a woman and do by a woman what God can do and has done. If a woman has a good husband, only God gave him to her. So, God has to be number one. Any man who wants to take a woman away from God and bring her to him is an insane man. A man is foolish to make a woman believe she must depend on him to teach her and pray for her. The best thing a man can do is get out of a woman's way and show her the way to God. When she gets there, thank God because when a woman is wrapped in God, a man's future is secure.

That is why I must say to the children of the Honorable Elijah Muhammad that Clara Muhammad was one of the most wonderful women who ever lived. The beauty of that woman's soul brought forth from the womb children and grandchildren who will be special in the world. A special woman creates special people.

The woman of Amran said, "My Lord, I vow to Thee." What does "vow" mean? When you make a vow, it is not only your desire. It is your will combined with your determination. Women should make this determination long before they become pregnant. Girls who have not known a man yet in their lives should put it in their minds that the world is in such a terrible condition because women who did not know their relationship to God brought forth men who are scourges to the planet.

One womb brought forth a Hitler, while another womb brought forth a Jesus Christ. One womb brought forth a Napoleon, Attila the Hun, and Tamerlane, while another womb brought forth a Moses, Abraham, and all the prophets of God. It is the womb of a woman. A woman can do it if she has the will to do it. Girls should say in their hearts, "What I produce from my womb, I vow to produce it for God. I pray that He will accept what my mind, operating on His Law, produces."

According to the Holy Qur'an, when the woman of Amran brought forth her child, "She said, 'My Lord, I have brought it forth a female. And Allah knew best what she brought forth." Men should not become excited when we want to see our image in our children, but women give birth to a female child. In the old Arab world, before Islam, fathers buried girls alive because they wanted male children who would be their heirs.

The Holy Qur'an says, "And the male is not like the female." He is letting us know that there is a difference, and God is He Who created the difference. Men should not think that because we are male, we are superior. We are great, but without the womb, we cannot advance beyond where we are. No matter how great a man is, he wants to produce something greater. The woman will do it for us if we give her a chance. The woman of Amran said, "My Lord, I've brought it forth a female. And the male is not like the female, and I have named it Mary. And I commend her and her offspring into Your Protection from the accursed devil."

She formed her child with a vow. Her desire to please God began writing on the brain of the child being fashioned from her blood. Women can make a child a mental giant or an imbecile. It is rooted in your thoughts and desires that write on the brain of the child. The child comes forward from the darkness of the womb with a predisposition toward a certain reality.

The Holy Qur'an continues, "So, Allah accepted her with a goodly acceptance and made her grow up a goodly growing and gave her into the charge of Zacharias. And whenever Zacharias entered the sanctuary to see her, he found food with her. He said, 'Oh Mary, whence comes this to thee?' And she said, 'It is from Allah. Surely Allah gives to whom He pleases without measure.'" After you have a good girl, you must put her in the charge of a good man—not a man who abuses his daughter, but a father who recognizes the sacredness of his daughter and the reverence for her womb and mind.

Mary grew up in the temple. The Honorable Elijah Muhammad was producing a nation of Marys. He grew the Black women in the Nation of Islam up in the temple under the Law of God. Whether women liked that law or not, he grew the woman up under that law. He taught us the right foods to eat and the impure things we should refrain from eating and drinking. He was purifying the woman's body and mind so that both wombs would deliver a child for God—not that in this generation we would see it, but in the future, we would see a new world come into existence from the wombs of women who dedicate their lives to God.

The angels said to Mary, "Oh Mary, surely Allah has chosen you, and purified you and chosen you above the women of the world." When God chooses a people for His Glory, He chooses the people, but He works mostly with the women because it is only through her womb that His Glory will be magnified. Men can do great things in their lives, but we will die one day. What difference does the greatness of a man make if the womb of his wife does not produce an advance over him in their children. The man would have lived in vain and will die without leaving any representation on the earth to carry on the good to which he dedicated his life. Men cannot make it without women. Our future is in the woman and through the woman.

The angels commanded Mary, "Oh Mary, be obedient to your Lord and humble yourself and bow down with those who bow. This is of the tidings of things unseen, which we reveal to you. And you were not with them when they cast their pens to decide which of them should have Mary in his charge." This is a decided decree.

Women were not there when the pens wrote what their wombs would bring forth. The Bible says I knew you. I was there before you were formed in the belly of your mother. I was with you. Jesus comes forth to change the world, save the world, and make the Kingdom of God a reality on earth, but he cannot do it without a woman.

The angels said, *"Oh Mary, surely Allah gives you good news with a Word from Him, of one whose name is the Messiah, Jesus, son of Mary. Worthy of regard in this world, and the Hereafter and of those who are drawn nigh to Allah. And he will speak to the people when in the cradle and when of old age, and he will be one of the good ones."*

And she said, *"My Lord, how can I have a son and a man has not yet touched me."* He said, *"Even so, Allah creates what He pleases. And when He decrees a matter, He only says to it, 'Be, and it is.' And Allah will teach him of the Book and the Wisdom and the Torah and the Gospel. And make him a messenger to the Children*

of Israel, saying, 'I have come to you with a sign from your Lord.'"
But it started with a womb and a woman saying, "I vow!"

22
The Glorious Act of Sex

Do you want to see the world delivered from this condition? Do you want it delivered? When you see the terrible condition of our people throughout the world, do you want to see this change? How bad do you want it? How much are you willing to sacrifice to bring about a change? How strong is your desire? Do you vow to do what is necessary to bring about this change?

When we get married, we say vows because we are determined to make the marriage work. We are not simply saying words. What do you do after your vow? Whatever God commands. His first command is, "Clean up!"

Men cannot produce good sperm with a dirty, filthy body filled with alcohol, cigarette tobacco, drugs, and filthy foods. We must clean up! We must get away from the fast food merchants of death. We must get away from drugs and medicine. Men must clean up their bodies so their sperm will be better sperm. Women must clean up their bodies so their eggs will be better eggs. We must begin there.

Jesus said, "I have come that you may have life and have it more abundantly." There was no Jesus in our lives until we met the Honorable Elijah Muhammad. We do not know how to live a long life. We were never taught. After we clean up, we must prepare for children. We should not just lie down and have children based on lust and passion. We must not let passion and lust become the core of the motivating force of thought that moves the sperm to contact the egg, lest our children have a predisposition to lust and filth.

We must change our thinking about sex. Sex is not lowdown and dirty, except we make it that way. Sex is a glorious thing. We should never engage in the act on a beast-like level. Sex is a responsible activity that is not the fruition of lust but the culmination of love. God intended sex to come after the development of natural love and affection. He did not intend for us to poison love and affection through experiencing lust. He did not intend for us to defile the human body and cripple the womb with lustful passion before we develop the natural love and seeking of each other and make a proper commitment to each other. The act of sex demands devotion.

When a woman finds the man of her choice, she should have gone through a process of trying to understand who this man is that she is about to choose to father her children. Women do not enjoy mothering a child for a man to whom she does not have a real connection.

When a woman really loves a man, she becomes consumed with him. Love is an overpowering force. It changes you. A woman wants to look like him. She takes on his speech pattern and many other characteristics of him. A woman gives herself to him willingly because she loves him. When that natural love is crushed, the second man never gets what the first man received from her.

Men should leave women alone if they do not mean women any good. If a man thinks a woman is ugly, does not like her, and only wants to use her, he should leave her alone—even if she is willing to throw herself at his feet. He should tell her to reverence her womb and tell her that she should not ever throw herself at a man who has not made a commitment to her. She will make excuses, but she will be ashamed.

A woman can become so hungry for a man's attention that she feels that if she does not give him her attention, maybe he will give his attention to another woman. She should let him give it to somebody else because her womb is too sacred. A woman should look a man over once, look him over twice, look him over thrice, and then maybe she will make the right decision when the right man comes along.

Mary said, "No man has yet touched me. I have not been unchaste." Isn't that beautiful? How many little Marys can say that? Everything in the Holy Qur'an is a principle that we should study. When Mary asked God how she could have a child since she had been chaste, He said, "All I have to say is 'Be,' and it is." Then the Holy Qur'an says, "And We sent to her Our Spirit, and it appeared unto her in the form of a well-made man."

When the Spirit of God comes in the form of a well-made man, a woman cannot turn him down. Even if she has loved before, that kind of man will make her love all over again, newer and deeper than she ever did. It will remind her of the first time she loved, but it will be even better because the Spirit of God is in the man. He means good by her. He will devote himself to her.

When he triggers that love, she will flame up in that love. Like a fire burns up old ideas, and like the phoenix bird, a new person comes up out of the ashes produced by the flaming fire of divine love. God is love. His Creative Power is manifest in true love.

When a man loves a woman and the woman loves him—and she has lived a clean life eating the right food and vowed with earnest desire in her prayers, "Allah, help me to produce from my womb a son or a daughter that will glorify You and change the reality of the world's condition. Bless my womb with substance." And repeats this prayer until the desire is in her blood, the cells of her brain and her egg. Then she meets him—she should hold herself back from him. No bedroom activity. No petting. No kissing on the lips. No breathing in the ear or biting on the neck.

The Bible says, "They tickle your ears with false doctrine." The ear is a strange thing. We like to hear compliments. That is like blowing in our ears. When a man blows in the ears of a woman, the room gets steamy. Then he drops down to her neck. In the Holy Qur'an, Allah says He is closer to us than our jugular veins. So, a man rests on a woman's jugular vein when he bites her neck.

By then, she has lost her resistance and becomes willing to give the man whatever he wants. Like Satan or Dracula, he starts taking the life force out of her, and she yields. Her knees open, and her secret parts are discovered. He laughs and walks away.

The Holy Qur'an says Allah gave us passion. Passion is not bad. We are all passionate, but the Holy Qur'an says we should restrain our passions except around those whom our right hands possess or those to whom we are married. Passion is good, but young people should restrain it. If they cannot restrain it, parents should keep watch because their ever-present vigil will restrain the passions of youth.

When a woman passionately loves a man, the act of sex is the culmination of that love. The woman looking to heaven and the man looking to the earth—this is very powerful. Her head with his head. Her chest to his chest. This spiritual love and electrical energy produced by that love creates a force field that energizes both parties and revives the mind.

When this act is done without love, devotion, or commitment, it degenerates both the woman and man. It is worthy for a woman to save herself for that wonderful person at the right time. When a woman has that kind of timing and that kind of person and finds out that she is pregnant—in fact, even before she becomes pregnant—she will want to produce life for him.

23
Elijah Muhammad

When a woman loves her husband, she is fashioning the child from him, but with God in mind. She must desire to produce a child that God will accept. She must humble herself to God. She must be a praying woman who bows down to God. This prepares her body and mind. Then, when she receives the good news of a pure child coming from her womb, we will not have to say, "Jesus is coming," because when women become like Mary, Jesus shall be in the world.

The Messiah's time is now! It is time for the world to be saved, but the wombs of women are not pure enough to bear the Messiah. If women knew that this is the hour that Jesus will come again, and he is the desire of all women, then women must desire now to bring Jesus back into the world. When you meet a man of goodness, lay down with him and produce the Messiah. He will speak wisdom from the cradle. When he is old, he will open the eyes of the blind and make the deaf hear and the dumb speak. By God's permission, he will raise the dead to life. Such a man came into the world, the Honorable Elijah Muhammad, from the womb of a blessed mother whose name was Maria.

When she was a young girl, she was told that she would bring forth a special child into the world. That blessed mother had 13 children. The Honorable Elijah Muhammad was her seventh child. As Elijah grew up, he was different from the other children. He only completed the fourth grade of school, but he studied nature. He would go to church, and his father would sit him on the mourner's bench while he preached.

His father was a Baptist preacher who would preach and fall out. His father had the spirit but not the understanding. Little Elijah said he knew what his father was preaching meant something else.

He said that one day when he grew up, he would preach, but he did not know what he would preach.

He grew from the womb of his mother. He has produced offspring, all of whom are valuable, including those children he produced from wives other than Sister Clara Muhammad given to him out of the Nation which he bore. We must understand another reality. We must lift our minds beyond the filth of a bedroom to see the working of God.

What was the quality of the wombs and thoughts of these women as they bore their children? How did their thoughts mark their babies either for the service of God or for damnation? Before you judge Elijah Muhammad, be careful. A man does not produce the kind of work he produced with the women of the Nation of Islam and then degenerate into a voluptuary.

Prophet Muhammad (peace be upon him) was blessed to have 11 wives. Allah (God) in the Holy Qur'an says that nine wives are sufficient. Why nine? How many planets are in the universe? The planets are all different. Even though different life grows on each planet, there is one sun that brings up different life on all the planets. From that nine and that one sun exists a common water that produces unlimited life. From the nine numerals, the "1" and the "0," we can make numbers to infinity.

From the nine wives and himself as the "1," he was going to produce a seed. From the womb of his mind and the wombs of women, he would produce a seed that is like the sands of the sea and the stars of the heavens; we would not be able to number them. God says, "Behold, I make all things new." He plans to destroy many people on the earth so that the earth can become a wide expanse to populate with the people of His choice. This is why the second Jesus is called the second Adam. God must give the second Adam a second Eve, who will be the mother of all new life.

IV
ELEVATION

24
Virtue and Chastity Build Character

Women have a profound role in the restoration and regeneration of a people. There is so much value in the woman. Allah (God) has given women power over the future of the nation. The profundity of the message is that women themselves have not been aware of their value in society. Because they are unaware of their value, they are abused and, unfortunately, abuse themselves.

The Honorable Elijah Muhammad was a man most of us did not understand, even those of us who followed him. Perhaps, it will take a lifetime to understand a man whom God has raised to make a change in the way of civilization—a change that can never be reversed. Because of his presence in the world, the Black man and woman will never, ever be the same again. A man of that profound consequence is not easy to understand. We are thankful to Allah (God) that we are yet alive to continue to reflect on him so we may better understand aspects of his life.

The Honorable Elijah Muhammad taught, "Where there are no decent women, there are no decent men, for the woman is the Mother of Civilization." The Honorable Elijah Muhammad taught, "A nation can rise no higher than its women." Yet, as Muslims, we are charged with a degree of male chauvinism.

Some Sisters did not understand why the Honorable Elijah Muhammad took them "out of the world" and asked them to cover their bodies. The Sisters did not understand why they should cover their hair. They did not understand why the Honorable Elijah Muhammad took so much time to reform the conduct of women— not only the way they walk but also the way they talk, the way they dress, the way they act in private, and the way they act in public. The Honorable Elijah Muhammad taught women the care of their hair, the care of their bodies, and the proper foods to eat.

He was passionately concerned with the reform of the Black woman because if there is no reform in the thinking of the Black woman, there cannot be any reform in the thinking of the Black man. The Honorable Elijah Muhammad said that 75 percent of his work was with women, and only 25 percent of his labor was with the man.

He never let a man go near the women's class. He would put out of the Nation any of his ministers who interfered with the women's class. He never let a man come into the class and teach women about themselves. He trained women to teach women and made their class so private that he forbade the women to discuss, even with their husbands, what was taught in their class.

Some Sisters felt that the Honorable Elijah Muhammad discouraged professional involvement because he did not wish to see them attend the White man's schools of higher learning—but not because he did not want higher learning.

One Brother sent his daughter to college, irrespective of what the Honorable Elijah Muhammad desired. The Honorable Elijah Muhammad told me to tell that Brother that if anything happened to his daughter while she was in the "devil's institution," the Honorable Elijah Muhammad would hold him thoroughly responsible. If she violated the Law of God while there, not only would she be punished, but the double punishment would come to her father.

What was the root of Elijah Muhammad's view of women? We cannot have ignorant women and smart men because women teach the male child and make them what they are for the future. If a woman is ignorant, she cannot produce brilliant children. Children will feed from their mother's breasts and feed from their minds. If there is nothing in a woman's head for them to feed on but the foolishness that the world teaches, then our future is jeopardized by the ignorance of the woman.

Why did Elijah Muhammad stop young women from attending the White man's universities and colleges? On the South Side of Chicago, he put up $1 million when he was considering purchasing what is now the South Shore Country Club and was going to buy it for $10 million. He entered into negotiations to buy the Tuskegee Institute in Alabama. In the *Muhammad Speaks* newspaper, he published his plan to build a 10,000-unit dormitory and the university level of Muhammad University of Islam on the land of the South Shore Country Club.

The city decided not to sell it to him, so they returned his $1 million. Today, the South Shore Country Club is simply a beautiful place, remodeled for dinner, dance, and partying, but not for the re-education of the Black man and woman so that we may take a proper and rightful place in society.

The Honorable Elijah Muhammad told me to tell my daughters that he was working on building the University level. If they would wait and be patient, he would put them in an environment that would protect the righteousness he had inculcated in them since they were girls. We do not find many virgins in this society, but most of the girls at the University of Islam were virgins. The Honorable Elijah Muhammad felt that the virtue of women and girls was more valuable than increased knowledge at the expense of their chastity.

Virtue and chastity build character in a woman, but education does not necessarily build their character. At Muhammad University of Islam, the hallmark of our educational system was building virtue and righteousness, along with building the minds of our young people. Every time we invest in our youth to build virtue and character, along with high degrees of education, we prepare a better future for ourselves. We have a lot of knowledge, but we do not have character. As a result, we are an immoral people with a multitude of degrees. We will lie, cheat, and steal. This is not good because we are only perpetuating the kind of world that Christ is coming to destroy.

If we want a better world, we cannot have a better world until we make better people. And we cannot make better people until we make a better woman. When we make a better woman, we have made a better people. So Elijah Muhammad sacrificed the higher learning of the Sisters to keep them in an environment of righteous conduct.

Some may ask why Elijah Muhammad didn't feel that the Sisters could hold themselves righteous in that environment after he had put righteousness in them. In hotels, they post a sign in the rooms: "Do not tempt the maids (or those who clean the rooms) by leaving your jewelry around." They are not saying that the maids are thieves, but why tempt them and make a thief out of them? So, guests are encouraged to put their jewelry in a safe place.

25
Projecting Will and Desire

Allah (God) says, in both the Bible and Holy Qur'an, that He created the heavens and the earth from nothing. The vast universe is a womb of space. His mind operated on that womb. He penetrated the darkness and saw what was in the darkness. He then projected His thoughts into the darkness and manifested His thoughts in reality. Every woman and girl should reflect on this. Every man should also reflect on this.

God was alone in the darkness of vast space. He had a vision in His brain of a light. He did not like the darkness. He wanted a light, but the light first was in His brain. He was a light of Himself. He wanted to produce a light after the light in His head. He said, "Be!" The word "be" does not mean that something magically pops up. God projects His desire into His Will. Then the forces, His Power, projected through His Will into space, manifest what is in His brain and bring it into reality.

The Honorable Elijah Muhammad said, "Whatever man can conceive in his brain, he has the ability to bring it forth into reality." The brain is a great place for us to operate. If we do not want anything, we will not get anything. We must first desire a thing before we get it. We must picture it in our minds. Then it satisfies the mind because the mind is satisfied with pictures. But the whole being is not satisfied until the picture in the mind becomes a tangible reality.

We usually work to bring into reality what we imagine. If we do not want anything out of life, we do not get anything out of life. As creatures of God, we have the power to project our will and envision what we want, and then go after it. We have the power to say, "Be," and go after it. We can take our will and desire, project them onto the womb, and bring into existence what we desire. How do we get in the right state to desire the right thing and then operate on it to make it so?

When the Honorable Elijah Muhammad called us out of the world and made us respect the Law of God, he put us in the frame of mind where the womb would produce a better product. We did not know why he told us he did not want us to smoke. He cleaned us up from alcohol, tobacco, and eating the wrong foods. He put men in the right physical frame to produce good strong sperm. He put women in a physical form to produce a good egg.

The egg in your ovary is no more than what you are. When you release it once every 28 days, that egg is a reflection of your thoughts and your diet, whatever you are. If you use drugs, crack, or chemical drugs—you may call it medicine—if you eat bad food, your egg is the product of yourself. If you do not have anything in your head of intelligence, when you learn that you are pregnant, you do not know what to do with yourself or the baby being made. You do not know how to make a baby properly. Whether you know it or not, your thoughts are projected onto the womb. So, what you are producing is of very little value. Before your children are born and after they are born, you are not projecting value into them because you do not have any value on yourself.

If God could make a light and say, "Be and it is," women can also be that powerful. When women get into the right frame of mind, they can produce mental giants from their wombs with a predisposition to master this life. We have done it accidentally. What if we did it on purpose?

26
The Science of Mating

A man is absolutely necessary not only because he has the sperm but because of how God created the woman. If a man is right, he can affect the quality of a woman's being. He actually turns her on and makes her vibrate to the Essence of God, Himself. The scripture says God is Love, not lust. What men are getting in our women are the leftovers.

A woman can only give her virtue once. She can only really love once. So, the only way that her love can come back to where it was when she first loved is that God, Who created her with that nature, comes into the man. When God is in a man, and that man touches a woman again in her life, she can love even more deeply than she ever knew it was possible to love because only God can turn on the divine spark of love in a woman.

When a woman first falls in love, that love is so pure that it causes her to give everything of herself to the object of her love. There is nothing of good or other than good that she would not do for that loved one. When she is disappointed by that love, it breaks her so completely that she gets a callous on her heart, like a sore, and she hardens. Once a woman is hurt in love, it is very difficult for her to love like that again. So, the man she ultimately commits to in a relationship never fully gets from her what she first gave freely. He has to work hard for years, but he may never get it.

Allah (God) is the Re-newer. He says He can reproduce creation as it once was. Only when we are touched by God, Himself, our Originator and Creator, that that newness of life and newness of love can return. Only in love that we find the Divine, Creative Force of God. When the right man comes into a woman's life, he triggers that essence again. The right man is not the man who is cute. The right man is not the man who has money. The right man is the man who has the Spirit of God in him. Without God's Spirit, a man is of no value. With God's Spirit, he becomes to the woman what the Originator intended him to be.

When a woman falls in love with a man like that, she desires to have a child for him. She wants to be there for him when he comes home. She wants to have him again. She wants to grow him up from her breast. She wants to nurse him at her breast and make him better than the man with whom she fell in love. When she gives birth to his son or daughter, she has the chance to make him over again and advance him into the future. Without love, she does not have the desire to make a better human being.

The Honorable Elijah Muhammad said, "A nation can rise no higher than its women." If women are not imbued with lofty ideals, they cannot bring children onto the earth imbued with lofty ideals. As Allah (God) looked at the womb of space and created from what was in His Mind and said, "Be and it is," a woman has the power to look at her womb and determine in her mind what she wants to produce. While she is forming the child, she is producing what is in her brain.

What is in a woman's mind is important for the advancement of a nation. So, the Honorable Elijah Muhammad thought more about protecting the virtue and chastity of women than putting them in institutions of higher learning where they would get higher knowledge but ruin their future with God by losing their virginity and ruining their virtue and chastity.

When a woman becomes pregnant, the preparation for forming that child is the cleansing of her body and mind, which the Honorable Elijah Muhammad did for us. By trying to live by the Law of God and eating the proper foods, we were in a better frame of mind to produce better children.

The Honorable Elijah Muhammad wanted us to have children. The more children we had, the more blessed we felt because we were trying to produce a better future. We did not worry about feeding them. We knew we would be able to feed them. We were prepared to work hard to prepare a future for our children, so we did not mind having them. By following the Teachings of the Honorable Elijah Muhammad, we accidentally produced beautiful children. But we must grow to the level of understanding of how to produce a better child scientifically.

The Honorable Elijah Muhammad taught us that there were three things that the White man never wanted to teach Black people: (1) the science of warfare, (2) the science of business, and (3) the science of mating. We must learn the science of choosing the proper mate so that we reduce accidents in producing good children. The White man knows how to produce thoroughbred horses and thoroughbred dogs. Don't you think he knows how to produce a thoroughbred human being?

They have not taught Black people the science of mating, so we are not careful in choosing our mates. We choose any person because what we want is a night of pleasure, not the furtherance of our people. When we get away from the pleasure principle and focus on the principle of procreation, we want to be careful in how we choose our mates.

The first verse that Allah (God) revealed to Prophet Muhammad was the verse of the 96th Chapter of the Holy Qur'an, entitled "The Clot." A clot is a lump of congealed blood that develops a few weeks after conception. The first revealed verse of the Holy Qur'an is the command to read. The verse says: "Read in the Name of thy Lord, Who creates man from a clot and taught man by the pen what man knew not." I read of a Japanese woman who produced four geniuses by beginning to read to her children while they were in her womb.

Once a woman discovers she is pregnant, she must begin to think about what she wants to do for God. Mary vowed that she would dedicate her child to God. If a woman does not vow before becoming pregnant that she will make her child for God to remove the scourge of what we see on the earth, she can never produce that kind of child. But if she starts vowing that she will produce a child for God, and cleanses her life, body, and mind, then she will be able to produce a child with a predisposition toward God and the regeneration of the people.

27
Following the Footsteps of Hagar:
How God Makes Us Rely on Him

Abraham's wife, Sarah, was barren, so Abraham went into her handmaiden, Hagar, who produced a child for him. Allah (God) called Abraham the father of the righteous, and Allah (God) is The Best Knower. Moses bears witness to Abraham. Jesus bears witness to Abraham. Muhammad bears witness to Abraham. God says that Abraham was a good man, yet circumstances in his life did not look good. Abraham was married to Sarah evidently for a long time. Abraham was not looking at any other woman. They are growing older, and they do not have an heir. So, Abraham approaches Sarah's handmaiden, and Hagar becomes pregnant with his child.

Later, God visits Sarah and tells her she will have a child. Although she laughs and tells God that she is too old, she gives birth to a child. The older child is Hagar's, but she and her child are put out of Abraham's house. She is running in the wilderness, and righteous Abraham is not taking care of her. According to the Bible, Hagar's child is named Isaac, but according to the Holy Qur'an, the child is named Ishmael.

In either case, Abraham has two children. If you were living during the time of Abraham, how would you view this circumstance since it is the man's responsibility to maintain the woman? Hagar is in the wilderness, running between two hills, trying to get food and water for her child. Hagar is ready to give up, and she lays her baby down. She is ready to die and let her baby die.

Then a well bubbles up at the foot of her child, the Well of Zam Zam, which has become a significant part of Islamic life. When Muslims make their sacred pilgrimage to Mecca [hajj], we have to retrace the steps of Hagar, not Sarah. Hagar was the woman put out of the house of Abraham. She appears to be the "illegitimate" wife and might be called a concubine. Yet, Muslims must retrace her steps.

Nevertheless, according to scripture, the covenant of Abraham was made with both Isaac and Ishmael. When Allah (God) wants to develop a woman and her offspring for Him, He puts her through trials so that she will have to call and rely on Him. Because she cannot find any man to maintain her, she has to call on God. When God is put in a woman, she does not lean on her husband. She leans on God. The more she leans on God and prays to God, the more her prayers go into her offspring.

My mother wanted to get rid of me early in her pregnancy. That thought is heavy in a woman's mind when trying to get rid of a child. My mother probably does not know how her thoughts affected me. As I grew older, I would not think much of myself. That made it easy for me to sacrifice my life for something bigger than myself. After my mother decided to keep me, she was troubled by my presence in her womb. She was so insecure over the circumstances of her pregnancy with me that she just prayed and prayed and prayed for God's deliverance. Her prayers went into me, and God's Hand was over her womb.

As a boy, I played games of security every night I went to sleep. I would see myself protected behind walls of steel, and nobody could get to me. Because my mother was so insecure in her pregnancy, I came from the womb insecure. But when I found the Honorable Elijah Muhammad and the God he represented, I found security. This is why I talk so boldly. I believe that the God of the Honorable Elijah Muhammad is strong enough to protect and defend me. Even though it does not look like I have any security around me, I feel secure in God.

The nature of a child originates from the womb. God will make a child rely on Him from the circumstances outside of the womb and the thinking of the woman.

28

Polygamy and the Seed of a Messenger

No man can be great if he is a womanizer. Yet the greatest of men had women around them who cultivated certain aspects of them, which broadened them.

David was called the Beloved of God, yet there were some circumstances in his life that we might not understand. One night while walking, David saw a beautiful woman, Bathsheba, in her tent, and he desired her. She was married to Uriah, one of David's soldiers who loved David immensely. When a battle arose, David sent Uriah to the frontline of battle, and Uriah was killed. David then gained access to Bathsheba. Although some may consider this horrible, Solomon was born from their relationship, the wisest man to come among the people of Israel.

Jesus had women around him. Some scholars read scripture and say Jesus had more than one woman. Others read scripture and say Jesus did not have any women at all. But Mary and Martha were always there, even when the male disciples were not. We do not read anywhere in scripture that Jesus was unclean in any way. He was completely a holy man.

Prophet Muhammad of Arabia was a lawgiver. He was the harbinger or the herald of a whole new civilization. In the Holy Qur'an, which is the final Revelation of God to this world before the Judgment, Allah (God) gives Prophet Muhammad permission to take nine wives. Women are not born into this world to share their husbands. If a man gets a woman into a polygamous situation, she is not happy, although some women may pretend to be happy.

In many ancient societies of the world, the chiefs had wives. In Africa, the chiefs and common men had wives. In Native American societies, the chiefs had wives. In Arabian society before Prophet Muhammad, men used women for pleasure without any responsibility for them. When Islam came, the Holy Qur'an said the common believing man could have up to four wives, but *only* under certain conditions and circumstances. The Holy Qur'an says that the rule is one woman for one man.

That is the best because a man cannot be just to many women. A man will find a favorite and be unjust to the other women he does not favor as much. This will create enmity and hatred among the women.

In a falling society with more women than men, women have become playthings for men. Many men are homosexual. Many are in prison. Many are in the armed forces because they cannot get a job. Women are left with a natural desire for a man, but there is not one for them.

Many women go to college and better their lives. They receive a good education but cannot find a man with whom they can hold a decent conversation that will attract their minds. They end up marrying because it is the right thing to do or because of a biological need. But they are not happy because a man cannot make a woman happy in bed. He has to make her happy in her head. If a man cannot reach a woman's mind, she will get tired of him in a short time. She will be sleeping with him, wondering if there is something better in life.

Women can produce the future and make it better, but there is no man to teach them right. If there is a man to teach them right, he is buried under so much rubbish that they cannot find him. The Honorable Elijah Muhammad's job was very hard, and he left us with a very hard job to do. With the Help of Allah, we will do it. In a society like this, the Holy Qur'an represents a healing. Sometimes we have to take medicine that does not taste good, but that medicine is good in the long run.

Polygamy is an ugly thing, not only in man's sight but it is ugly in the sight of God. It is not as ugly as adultery, fornication, prostitution, lesbianism, or homosexuality. Polygamy is a sin. It is not the norm, but God uses it to bring a society back to balance when the balance is destroyed. Women do not want to share their husbands with another woman, and they have a right. Women sacrifice so much already for a nation. But the sacrifice of their husbands is the most painful of all for a woman to make.

Nevertheless, it is a decision that women will be called on to make in the future. It will be painful, but we will never get free until we fight, bleed, and die like all other oppressed people on the earth. The freedom of our people is not going to come without a fight. The Honorable Elijah Muhammad would recite this to me when I would sit at his table: *"Can you go to heaven on flowery beds of ease while others fought to win the prize and sail through bloody seas? If I must reign, I too must fight and sail through bloody seas."* Then he gave us a Fight Song, "We are fighting for Islam, and we will surely win."

I have a beautiful wife and children. If I am killed for the sake of the truth, I would expect one of my Brothers—not one who is poor, ragged, naked, hungry, and out of doors, but one who has some money—to look after my wife and children. Since I have gone to the grave, I can no longer comfort my wife. I would expect one of my Brothers to love me enough to help rear my children. But if all men have in their minds is sex and orgies, then men have the wrong thought. Allah (God) cannot use a filthy and dirty mind. The polygamy mentioned in the Holy Qur'an is not a filthy thing. It is not made for filthy people. It is made to correct an imbalance in society.

Abraham was an example. Allah (God) wanted to produce something from the Seed of Abraham. When He chooses a man of consequence, He chooses that man's seed. That man's seed grows as he grows. It matures as he matures. If Allah (God) does not waste even a leaf of a tree, Allah (God) cannot waste the righteous seed of His Servant.

Abraham was old, but he could still produce sperm. His wife Sarah was barren, so Hagar produced a child for him. Hagar was put out in the wilderness, which made Hagar a stronger woman. She ran in the wilderness without any man to look after her. The thoughts of God served as her protector in her brain. She could have produced an offspring that hated Abraham if she had negative thoughts against him and said negative things about him. Since she had positive thoughts about him, she produced a child who, regardless of the condition, loved his father and the God who provided nourishment for his mother while she was running in the wilderness.

29
The Domestic Life of the Honorable Elijah Muhammad

The Honorable Elijah Muhammad was born of a woman named Maria. When she was a girl, she was given a vision that she would produce a child of great consequence in the future. Her seventh child was named Elijah, and he was an unusual child. He grew up in the church with his father, who was a Baptist minister. He grew up desiring to understand the Bible that his father preached. As a boy, he knew he would preach one day, but he felt he would preach a little differently from his father, although he did not know what he would preach.

The womb of his mother was blessed with him, and he was born with a predisposition and inclination toward higher wisdom. He only completed the fourth grade yet studied nature and everything around him while he grew up in Georgia. He had a mule that studied, and he could get the mule to do things that his brother could not get the mule to do. His brother would beat the mule, but Elijah would whisper in the mule's ear, and the mule would work for Elijah. Elijah Muhammad did not want his brother to beat his mule. He did not know that, years later, he would have to work with a mule people. He did not know that his study of nature and animals was the preparation for him to trap and tame a wild people and make us civilized.

In Detroit, Michigan, in 1931, he met a very Wise Man, Master Fard Muhammad. After Elijah Muhammad heard Master Fard Muhammad, he instantly changed. When he returned home to his family, it was as though something had worked magic on him. His wife immediately noticed the change Master Fard Muhammad had produced in him.

Elijah reacted in this manner because, from the womb, he was born to meet this Man. From the womb, he was looking for someone to help deliver his suffering people. When he found that Man, he became one with that Man in a spiritual relationship. This is the power of the womb and the power of the mind, which is another womb.

In Elijah Muhammad, Master Fard Muhammad saw a womb He could impregnate with truth. In a majestic way, Elijah Muhammad would take what Master Fard Muhammad had given him and produce a nation. After 40 years of work, the Honorable Elijah Muhammad produced that which Black people in America had never seen before and that which was never seen anywhere on the earth.

The kind of man and woman Elijah Muhammad produced is absolutely a phenomenon. The Honorable Elijah Muhammad is an unusual man. He is an extraordinary man. A man who could do this for so many people is a man imbued with the Spirit of God. A time came when a condition in his personal life would severely try his family and the Nation of Islam.

He met his beloved wife Clara Evans before being called to this Word. She was a beautiful Black woman, and he fell in love with her, and she with him. From a very young age, they grew together. She saw him while he was down and mentally dead, and she saw him in his resurrection.

The Honorable Elijah Muhammad lived a decent life for 25 or 30 years, where he did not look at any woman other than his wife, although women constantly looked at him and laid traps for him. While on the run for seven years, he taught prostitutes in their homes but never laid with them. He was a clean man, a righteous man, a good man, and a one-wife man because he loved the Law of God. He has a nature like other men. But for a man to be a great man, God must inspire him with the strength to put his nature under control.

There has been much misunderstanding about the domestic life of the Honorable Elijah Muhammad. When he was in his 50s, he took on wives. In the 33rd Chapter of the Holy Qur'an, which deals with the life of Prophet Muhammad, God gives him permission to take wives. Muhammad was afraid. He did not want to do this for fear of what it would produce in his community because he knew what he had taught them.

Allah (God) says in the Holy Qur'an, "Why do you fear to take what I have made lawful to you?" Some of us fear men as we ought to fear Allah. The Honorable Elijah Muhammad knew that when the knowledge of his domestic life became public, it would affect his wife, children, and followers. It could destroy all the years of work he had built on a base of righteousness. But if Allah (God) ordered him to do that, and he did that, Allah Himself would protect the Nation.

Children are being made from a negative circumstance, and every one of those children—of a righteous mother and a righteous father—had a role to play in the Nation of Islam's development. The Honorable Elijah Muhammad said that role was more so after he was gone than while he was present. After he was gone, they would fully come into the understanding of this aspect of his life that was so painful to the whole family.

Mother Clara Muhammad endured excruciating pain. When she passed, the Honorable Elijah Muhammad cried profusely at the funeral. He loved his wife and knew that this wife, more than anyone else, was with him from the beginning. He would not want to do anything to hurt her. She did not like this aspect of the Holy Qur'an because it is natural for a woman not to like the fact that this great man of hers had to be shared with others for a purpose bigger than her concern as a loving wife.

His seed is so powerful that the Honorable Elijah Muhammad said to us one night, *"A man like me will never be in the future, and a man like me has never been before."* He is a man so critical to the rise of the Black nation that his germ cannot be relegated to a woman who lost her ability to bear children, but he is growing in wisdom and stature.

The scripture says Lot went into his daughters, but no righteous prophet of God will go into his daughter; that is incest. This scripture means that when a messenger spiritually fathers people, they are like his children. The women who became wives of Muhammad and mothers of his children were daughters to him because he fathered them in the Truth. He reared them up into the love of that Truth, and they loved him as the Messenger of that Truth. Many of these women were not thinking of Elijah Muhammad in a romantic way, though some were. But it is the Spirit of God in a man that attracts women. That is natural and normal. That is a prerequisite to help reform women in the way of God and His Servant.

Elijah Muhammad called every one of the wives "Aisha." Aisha was the wife who ended up with Prophet Muhammad. He started with one, Khadija, and in the end, he died in the tent of Aisha. Aisha had certain qualities that were loved by Prophet Muhammad. Elijah Muhammad calling each of his wives this name looks very deceitful on the surface. On a deeper level, he did not know which one would end up as Aisha, so he gave all of them the noble title to live up to the name.

If the Honorable Elijah Muhammad was a man who only wanted sexual partners, he could have had sex without having children. But children were born from his wives. A child can be hidden but for so long. Although the White man calls his children illegitimate, there is nothing illegitimate about his children. There is a higher law than the White man and his law that can legitimize a child. If Elijah Muhammad runs from his responsibility to care for the mothers and the children, then he makes his children non-legitimate by his actions. But they came here legitimately, by the Law of God and not by the law of the White man. God's law says the prophet can have nine wives. So, if he believes he is the Messenger of God, he should take wives and care for them and their children.

If a more profound understanding of the domestic life had been taught, the Believers would have understood it. Aspects of it are so critical that it may take a much deeper study to understand because the thing that we think is mud is the very thing that will purify us. The Holy Qur'an says, "Go to the mud and purify yourself." In the domestic life of the Honorable Elijah Muhammad is a purifying agent because that knowledge brought out all the things hidden in our hearts that we did not even know were there.

It was necessary to produce children from the second set of marriages of Elijah Muhammad. God allowed Muhammad nine wives. There are nine planets. Each planet shows a different color. Each color has a different meaning. Each planet has different water. Each planet brings up a different life, all generated from the light from one great sun. From the numbers one to nine and zero, we can make numbers into infinity.

So, God gives the prophet nine wives, and the prophet becomes a light-giving sun, a Messenger of Truth. Each wife who was blessed to produce life, the light from them is different, but all of the children were beneficial for the Nation. Beginning with the children of Mother Clara Muhammad, not one of the children of Elijah Muhammad is dumb. Every one of them is intuitively smart.

No matter what they are doing with their lives, they have abilities right now that the Nation needs to grow strong. They have valuable knowledge to give to the Nation. They are in the arts, science, computers, law, banking, finance, medicine, and all kinds of fields. Even though it grieved the Honorable Elijah Muhammad, he followed the command of God in order to produce something for the future of the Nation of Islam.

Elijah Muhammad prayed that the wombs of his wives would produce children who would grow up and become gods— not Allah, but masters of their fields of endeavor. It is time for us to have a more mature understanding of the life of Elijah Muhammad. It is time for us not to only focus on the pain of the wives or the first wife, but we ought to focus on his pain.

He loved deeply, but he simply got to the point where he steeled himself and said, "You can take it or let it alone. You are either with me or against me. After I have shown you all that I have shown you, if you do not think Allah is with me, then leave me." Allah is still with him, though he is gone physically from among us.

The words that he said are still coming to fruition. There is nothing for us to do but come together as one family and bring his family back together. As one mighty Nation of Islam, we will effect the rise of all 30 million of our people and reform the Islamic world.

30
Think About the Future

God has blessed the womb of the Black woman of North America. After receiving this message, women should think about the future and the children they will bear. Women must start cleaning up their lives.

Do not smoke—not because I say so or because religion says so. We should not smoke because it kills our lungs, health, and blood. Do not drink because it ruins our liver and health. We will make sinews and flesh of a new life that we will cripple by how we live our lives.

Women should not let any man get to them. If he does not mean her any good, she should leave the man alone, regardless of his looks. Until she finds out a man's intentions, a woman should not have sexual relations with him. Women are sacred and should begin acting like they are sacred. We should stop thinking that pleasure is all there is to life because that pleasure has brought women much pain and hurt.

We should pray that Allah (God) blesses our women and girls to see their responsibility to make a better future by making better men. They cannot make better men unless they produce them from their wombs. Women must be wise and give themselves to the study of knowledge. Women must cut out the frivolity. It is alright to dance and party, but they cannot be frivolous women who party all the time. Women must become more dignified if they are going to bring children of consequence onto the earth.

Until we lift women, we are not going to create a great nation or a great civilization. Catholics pray, "Hail Mary, full of grace, the Lord is with thee." "Hail" is a word of praise, honor, and elevation. When a righteous woman is full with a child, that is the Grace of God being born into the world to change the reality of the way we live. "Hail Mary, full of grace, God is with you. Blessed art thou among women and blessed is the fruit of your womb, Jesus."

If a woman wants to produce a righteous giant, she should study Maryam, the mother of Jesus. Chapter 19 of the Holy Qur'an is given to her. If women study their lives and pattern their lives after her life, we will change the world.

V
TRANSFORMATION

31
The Struggle of Marriage: The Unity of Two Souls

The key to raising our people out of this condition is our women. The Honorable Elijah Muhammad taught where there are no decent women, there are no decent men, for the woman, particularly the Black woman, is the Mother of Civilization. The Honorable Elijah Muhammad also taught no nation can rise any higher than its women.

In Proverbs, Solomon says, "A wise child maketh a glad father, but a foolish child is the heaviness of its mother." If you have an ignorant woman, more than likely, she will produce children after her own kind. Whatever a woman is, that is what she will produce. If the nation is going to be elevated, then women must be lifted. If the nation is going to be a wise nation, then women must give themselves to the acquisition of knowledge. If the nation is going to be reformed and advanced, then the Black woman today has to give herself to be reformed.

As long as our women are in a low condition, we will always produce men who are in a low condition. Women are not happy with the kind of men we have today and reject them. Mothers are not pleased with the men they have raised. Society must take its responsibility, but mothers must take the full weight because the scripture says, "Train a child up in the way it should go, and when it is old, it will not depart from that way."

If mothers put the right knowledge in their children, society cannot take it out. The right knowledge has been absent from the mind of the Black woman and the Black man. From generation to generation, we keep repeating history and do not make new steps as a people.

The Honorable Elijah Muhammad said that 75 percent of his work was with the woman. Only 25 percent was with the man because when you teach a man, you teach an individual, but when you teach a woman, you teach a nation. When you reform a man, you reform an individual, but when you reform a woman, you reform a nation.

Marriage is a key institution if we are going to build a strong family. If we are not concerned about family, then we are not concerned about our people and nation. If we have a weak family, we have a weak nation. If we have a strong family, we have the potential for a strong nation. A strong family is only built upon a strong relationship between the male and the female, called husband and wife.

The union of male and female is called *nikah* in Arabic, which means "the uniting." When two people agree to marry, they are not agreeing that they are, in fact, married. They are agreeing that they are mutually compatible, and they desire to travel life's road together. They solemnize their intention in a marriage ceremony. It does not say that they are, in fact, united. It solemnizes their intention to struggle for that unity.

Unity is a word easily spoken, but it is difficult to achieve. The union of sperm with ovum that begins life is a very difficult journey and process. It is a sign of the difficulty faced by a male and a female who intend to be one and work at it until they make it so. Unfortunately, many people enter marriage with the back door in mind. They think they will get out of it if it does not work. Or they tell a friend they will leave the first time their spouse messes up. These people should never marry.

Prophet Muhammad said, "Marriage is one-half of faith." This is very powerful. Marriage is one-half of faith. Faith is that hope and spirit that makes an individual journey towards the Creator to find oneness with God. Paul said, "Faith is the substance of things hoped for, the evidence of things unseen." The real aim of life is to come on the earth from sperm mixed with an ovum, to begin a journey that does not stop once we come forward out of our mother's womb. It does not stop when we get a Master's or doctorate degree. It does not stop until the soul of the one born into the world becomes united with the essence of the Creator, and they become as one.

Then the Holy Qur'an says, "O soul that is at rest, well-pleased and well-pleasing." It is beautiful to become well-pleased with God and well-pleasing to God because we struggled all our life with the vicissitudes, trials, and tribulations of life to become one with God, and we finally made it. That is a blessing.

Marriage is one-half of that journey. Any man or woman who will quickly walk out on marriage will quickly walk out on the struggle to become one with God. We say for better or worse in our vows, but many really mean only for better. We say for richer or poorer in our vows, but many really mean they will stay married if we get some money. We say in sickness and health, but many mean as long as their spouse stays healthy, they will stay but do not intend to care for an invalid.

The journey to God is wrought with danger. So many people say they love God. But to walk toward God, we must walk through difficulty and opposition and struggle with ourselves to overcome our weaknesses. Sometimes we say it is not even worth it and give up. The greatest struggle is the struggle to unite with God. Second to that is the struggle with our mates that we have chosen.

If we can make it with our mate, we are halfway on our journey to God, so says Prophet Muhammad. How many people were married last year and are still married? Some marriages do not last beyond six months. They let the marriage get cold, stale, and dead and began grumbling and fighting. Finally, they both gave up and left. Children are left torn and divided, not wishing to choose between their mother and father. Loving both but, unfortunately, had to choose because their parents did not struggle at the most difficult time in marriage. They might have been able to save their marriage if they had the right attitude when they entered matrimony.

Marriage is a struggle. It is not easy. It is not lying in bed and enjoying each other sexually. Marriage is the sincere struggle of two souls to unite, not two bodies. Bodies can unite instantly, but the union of souls makes the union of bodies truly joyful. When the two parties in a marriage become dissatisfied with each other, the spirit of love is reduced according to the level of argument—the more argument in a marriage, the more dissatisfaction. The more dissatisfaction, the more the loss of the spirit of love. When no love is left, there is nothing on which to base a marriage.

The Holy Qur'an says Allah hates divorce. Yet so many people today get divorced. If we are sincere and wish to make our marriages work, if we struggle hard enough, God will help us overcome the difficulty because He hates divorce and wants to encourage the union of the male and female.

32
The Womb Can Advance Our Liberation

We have been ruined as a people. There is no sense in talking about liberation or the racist institutions of America and then coming home and degrading our women. If men use women and throw them out like toilet tissue, then we really do not want liberation because liberation is a process. It is not a one-generational thing. We may liberate to a degree, but the womb of a woman can advance the cause of liberation much further.

No matter what a man has gained in his lifetime, a woman can produce a child for him that will go further than him, with his desires and the woman's desires at the root of that child. But when a woman is destroyed and does not know what to do with the life in her womb, she will eat the wrong foods, drink the wrong drinks, smoke death, and put crack in her veins at the same time she is forming the brain cells of a new life. She is killing the future because she does not know how to protect the future. The man is only a one-dimensional, pleasure-seeking animal who lives for today and makes no thought for tomorrow.

Jesus said, *"Take no thought of what tomorrow will be."* But tomorrow is built on today. Women are today, but they are also our tomorrow. If women do not take care of themselves today, then we have no tomorrow. A woman does not need a man to love her in order to love herself and do good by herself. Abusing a woman is dangerous.

When we rebel against God, we pay a price for that, and the price of rebellion is death. The form that death comes is that we produced a life on this earth that cannot get over 60 or 70, or even over 40 years old. Death pervades our community. It is not just that the White man is putting death in the community. It is that we gravitate toward death.

Suppose the White man had rats skewered and posted shops up and down the street, and he said, "Delicacy: Harlem Super Rats." You would walk by him, wouldn't you, because you do not have an appetite for that? But the White man has crack up and down the street, and we buy it. What gives us an appetite for crack? What gives us an appetite for alcohol? What gives us an appetite for cigarettes, tobacco, and reefer that is destroying our health and mind? It is because we are on a course bent on self-destruction and suicide. Suicide is the killing of self. It is the height of self-rejection, self-hatred, and self-negation.

If a woman is having a baby and does not want it, the very thought of "I do not want you" will be put in the child. The child comes forward and looks like any other baby, but it has a predisposition that makes it difficult for the child to accept the value of its life.

Even if the woman tried to get rid of the child by sitting in a hot tub of water, taking quinine and all the old remedies for aborting a child, and could not kill the child, murder was still in her mind. The mother is a murdering and lying mother; and lying and murder are in the womb. She projects it from her mind right into her womb. The baby comes out with a predisposition to lie, steal, and murder.

We have produced a generation of liars, thieves, and murderers that are now consuming our flesh and blood as though they were programmed like robots to destroy their communities, families, mothers, and fathers. Men did this by not caring for women. Men did this by calling women b----s and treating women like b----s. Men did this by calling women dogs and turning the process of making a God backward.

33
Coming out of Triple Darkness: The Universe is a Womb

Women are in such a bad condition today that they perpetuate their own destruction. A man does not have to put a woman down anymore. She puts herself down.

Women are difficult to reform. Even though they know a change must be made, they do not want to change. Some women have loved a man that they grew to hate. Women have children in the world that may look like their fathers because they were conceived in a day of lust, but now women are constantly feeding their children hatred for the source of their life germ.

Sisters, the Honorable Elijah Muhammad taught us, and the Holy Qur'an bears him witness, that we are supposed to reverence the womb that bore us into this world. To reverence the womb means to hold the womb in deep respect and awe because the womb is majestic. It is the laboratory where God, Himself, operates. The Honorable Elijah Muhammad taught how Allah (God) created Himself. Allah (God) neither begets nor is begotten. If He was not begotten and He is the Living God, how did He get here? He was Self-created.

The Honorable Elijah Muhammad said God came "out of triple darkness." This means that the universe was a womb for Him. He returned to that womb to create everything that was in His Mind. He is a Mighty God. The Holy Qur'an says all Allah (God) has to say is "cum fia cum" or "Be, and it is."

Allah (God) examined the darkness of space. In His Mind, He saw the sun as a thought. Then He said, "Be," and brought it out of the womb of space. The sun is there. The moon is there. The stars are there. It all came from nothing. That is how God uses the womb. That is why we call the universe "she." The universe is pregnant and always bringing forth new things.

How dare women think they are nothing when (Allah) God blessed them with a double womb. He blessed women with a mind that is a womb, and He blessed them with a physical reality that is a womb. Then He makes you a co-operator with Him and an assistant to Him, if you will, in forming that which is in the womb.

Hitler is a product of the womb. Attila is a product of the womb. Napoleon is a product of the womb. Jesus is a product of the womb. Muhammad is a product of the womb. The difference lies in the mothers who bore these children.

If we reflect on these words and internalize them, they will make us want to change.

34
Correcting the Conditioning of the Womb

There are three stages in the development process. The first is the preparatory stage before gestation. The second is the gestation period, where a woman is pregnant and developing. The third is after birth, which is the process of nursing. These three stages are interrelated, and they are powerful.

Men must realize that the sperm we carry is the future. The head of the sperm is like a computer ingrained with all kinds of information from past eons. That is why Solomon could say there is nothing new under the sun because, for everything that is created, there is a record of it. The record is in the sperm. When the sperm is emitted, that sperm has the potential to grow to master this life, but it must be nurtured properly.

Teenagers are already ruining their lives because they do not understand their connection to the future. They must understand right now that they have to start building the tissues, blood, and bone of their bodies, which is the future of our people. If you love your people, you do not want to produce a weak specimen. You want a strong child.

You cannot have a strong child if you put poison into your body. It is a sacred vessel. When you smoke, thousands of poisons in the cigarette become a part of you. Therefore, it becomes a part of the sperm. As smoking and drinking weaken the human being, smoking and drinking attack the head of the sperm, which carries the genetic coding for the new life.

All a wise scientist has to do to destroy our future as a people is continue to feed you cigarettes, alcohol, crack, marijuana, pork, poisoned chemical products, denatured food, and canned goods that do not have any life in them. The more we eat these products, ingest them, and digest them, we kill not only our brain power and our beauty. We also kill our future by making the sperm as weak as water.

Girls should prepare their bodies for the future. Do not eat improper foods, drink improper drinks, or fill the beautiful form of their bodies with garbage. The more we poison our bodies, eventually it will affect us. By the time females reach puberty, they already have eggs destined to be weaklings because they did not nurture themselves from the best part in the earth but nurtured themselves from filth and debris. We can only produce from that which we nurse ourselves.

During the preparation stage, we must clean up. When the Honorable Elijah Muhammad put us under the Restrictive Laws, if you were caught smoking, you received 90 days out of the mosque; for drinking, 90 days; fornicating or committing adultery, one to five years. We thought it was terrible that he put such a strict law on us. The minute he was gone, and it looked like the law was relaxed, our behavior became crazy because we did not want to be held that tight under the law. When it looked like Imam Warithudeen was not going to be strict with us, we liked him. We did not like his father because he held us tight. What was Elijah Muhammad producing?

The Honorable Elijah Muhammad taught that there are three sciences that the White man will never teach Black people. For us to be great on the earth, we must master these three sciences, which are primary sciences. One of them is the science of warfare. The White man does not ever want Black people to know how to engage in warfare. Whatever we build with the science of warfare, he will never be able to take it away. Without this knowledge, however, whatever we have built, he has taken away from us.

Another science is mating. Do you think the White man knows how to produce a thoroughbred dog and a thoroughbred horse yet does not know how to produce mental giants? He knows how but he will not teach Black people. What does it mean when the doctor in Yacub's history took a sample of the blood and said the blood does not match? The secrets of our lives are in our blood. You can say you are clean and have never used any drugs. But when we examine your blood, we can tell your habits from your blood because your blood is your essence. It is your life.

When we become scientists at mating, we have to check the life of the man or woman we want to marry. You know it will not work from the beginning if there is no compatibility. You reject her; you reject him. The more we mature, we will understand this science. For now, we accidentally produce giants from the womb and are fascinated. It is just that Allah (God) put His Hand over the womb. Sometimes even though the mother is crazy, He still puts His Hand over the womb and gives her a very special child.

35
Love is the Creative Force of God

When that right man comes along, Sisters, you will know it because the Spirit of God in him will resurrect in you the love that died when you got hurt. A husband cannot produce good, strong babies, turning over with lust for his wife. If she tells you she is not interested in having sex, you must respect her. She has feelings. You cannot take from her. She has to give. If she does not give, do not take because that baby will be formed in a resisting womb.

There is nothing filthy about sex. It is only what we bring to it. It is not a dirty thing. It is a glorious thing. It is God's natural way. He set it up for us, and that is the way He wants human life procreated. But there is a science to mating. It is not supposed to be accidental. When a listless woman, who does not want to be bothered sexually by her husband, finds out that she is pregnant, she will produce a listless child who does not want to do anything.

If you want a child filled with life and power, do not let the love die between you and your spouse. There is nothing more powerful than the embrace of two people who are genuinely in love. The energy in love is the creative force.

The Bible says God is Love. If God is love, that is the creative force. That is the energizing force. To have sex without love is degrading to both parties. You can never bring to sex the energy or the high level of passion. The Holy Qur'an is not against us showing passion, male and female. But it says that you should restrain your passions except with those to whom you are married. It did not say you should be cold.

When love is present between two people, the tenderness of love culminates in an act of the expression of that love. That act is a totally reviving and creative act. Imagine a man and woman who genuinely love each other, not lust after each other. The fire and passion in their embrace create the force that will project the sperm with the life of God in it.

That is why pregnancy should be planned. If a couple decides they want to produce a child who will change the condition of the world, then they must prepare themselves to forge a new way. The man must woo the woman all over again until the love for each other is very strong.

During this period, everything you put in your mouth must be pure. Everything you put in your mind must be good. You must start weeding thoughts of envy, jealousy, and bitterness from your mind because you are now going to bring to birth the Messiah.

"Hail, Mary." They said, "Jesus is coming." When is he going to get here? When we all get our acts together, Jesus will be present. A real Jesus is coming, but we can produce him on our level. Both parties must clean up until they believe it is time to conceive. The best time to plant the seed of life is not during the night in the wee hours when you are tired, and the sun is down. The best time to plant the seed of life is during the time of the rise of the morning star.

Jesus said, *"I am the Seed of David, the root of Jesse, the bright and the morning star."* You want to conceive life when the sun is coming up in the East, and the energy is in you from a night of rest and sleep. Then the two mates, with love and passion, can come together, bearing witness to the greatness of God.

36
The Parable of 19

One of the foremost prayers in Catholicism is "Hail Mary." Muslims may reject such honor and adulation, but we should deal with this from the view of the Holy Qur'an. In one sense, Catholics and Christians have taken this honor to the extreme. In another sense, Muslims have rejected it to the extreme. So, both religions are in trouble today. Catholics abuse and misuse women. Muslims, by their non-use, abuse, and misuse women. Neither the Catholic nor Muslim world is worth anything when it comes to women.

It does not have anything to do with Jesus or Prophet Muhammad. Prophet Muhammad was for the liberation of women, but Arab culture has been superimposed on the Teachings of the Holy Qur'an. Today, women are catching hell in an Arab culture that attributes this mistreatment to Islam.

In the Holy Qur'an, the 19th Surah is entitled "Maryam." It is the only chapter in the Holy Qur'an given the name of a specific woman. Why would Allah (God) reveal the most powerful of all books ever to be revealed and name a chapter after a woman, and He did not name it after Muhammad's mother? He did not name it after Abraham's mother. He did not name it after the mother of Noah, Lot, or Moses. He named the chapter after the mother of Jesus. In all Arabic writings, when you call a man's name, you say, "Muhammad ibn Abdullah" or "Muhammad, the son of Abdullah" or "Yusef ibn Shah" or Yusef, the son of Shah." But when you mention the name of Jesus, you say, "Esau Ibn Maryam Al Mafiq" or "Jesus, the son of Mary." Why mention Mary and not Joseph?

Why is the chapter the 19th Surah and not the 20th, 15th, 14th' or 100th? Nineteen is a secret number in Islam. The scholars and scientists in Islam are wrangling over the Parable of 19. There is a one and a nine. When you put them together, you have 10. Maryam, 19, the Lord is with you. There are nine planets. Every planet has a different color and different water. Every planet brings up a new kind or form of life from the power of one sun. The "Big Ten" in astronomy refers to the sun and her nine planets. In Arabic, the sun translates as *Al-Shams* and is called "she." She: Maryam. "Hail, Mary, full of grace."

If we are going to be liberated in the future, it will come through the woman. Our fall came through the woman. Our rise will have to come through the woman. What kind of woman was Mary, and what kind of child did she produce?

The third Chapter of the Holy Qur'an, entitled "The Family of Amran," has a very serious and beautiful verse. A woman of Amran says in prayer to God, *"My Lord, I vow to you what is in my womb to be devoted to your service, so accept it from me."*

When Abraham and Ishmael rebuilt the foundation of the Kabbah, they prayed, *"Our Lord, show us our way of devotion and turn to us mercifully."* Abraham asked God to accept the work that he and Ishmael had done on the foundation of the house. They were dealing with stone and prayed to God to accept their work on stone. Here is a woman telling God, *"I vow what is in my womb to You."* That is where it starts.

A vow is a declaration of intention or desire backed by the power of will. The woman of Amran said to God: I vow, with all the power of my being, this that is in my womb. I vow it to You and ask You to accept it from me. I vow it to Your service.

Women have a right to love us, men, even though it is a weak right because we have not done well by our women. Not because we did not want to do good, we just did not know how. Women could forgive us for our wickedness and ignorance, but who protected you all this time, Sisters? Without any man by your side, who looked after you? It was a mighty God.

Your vow is not to a man, even though you conceived life from his sperm. Your vow is to God. You should say, like the woman of Amran, "I vow what is in my womb to You, and I ask You to accept it." The Holy Qur'an says: *When she brought it forth, she said: My Lord, I have brought it forth a female—and Allah (God) knew best what she brought forth—and the male is not like the female, and I have named it Mary, and I commend her and her offspring into Thy protection from the accursed devil.*

During the time of Prophet Muhammad, Arabs were killing female children because most men did not think a female child had any value. They wanted a male child. This verse in the Holy Qur'an shows that when the woman of Amran brought forth what she had vowed, it was a girl. She made that girl from the womb because her intention, desire, and will were in her vow. This demonstrates how to make a good baby.

Allah (God) pulls out of the universe what is out there and makes it according to His Will. A woman can take the seed of a common man. He does not have to be a brainiac. He simply has to have enough brains to give his seed to you. You must have enough brains to know what to do with it.

A blank piece of paper, like a dollar bill, only has value because of what is impressed upon it. Likewise, your child is like a blank piece of paper. From your mind, you can impress upon it what you vow. A common mother, without much skill and wisdom, who knows how to love God enough to impress on that child the thoughts of a vow can erase the condition surrounding the baby while it is being formed. You will never miss if you eat the right foods and try to think the right thoughts. Every baby born will be born from the womb, a potential giant. It is you. Hail, Mary.

37
A Well-Made Man

The woman of Amran vowed from her womb, and Mary came forth. She did not look like she was disappointed. She commended that daughter into the hands of a righteous man. When you produce a nice daughter, sometimes the man cannot keep himself from his own daughter. Men, if you want to destroy the future, abuse your children. If you want to ruin a young girl who loves you purely, try to have sex with her. If you do that, you will destroy the good work of a fine mother.

The work of a good mother must be that the child must grow up in the hands of a guardian who will protect that child. Mary was put into the hands of Zacharias. Mary grew up in the temple. Every time they went into the temple to see her, there was food around her. They said, "Mary, how do you have this food in here?" She said, "My Lord provides, and He is the best of providers." This has deep significance.

When the Honorable Elijah Muhammad taught Black women and put them in the Muslim Girls in Training class, they were women put in his charge. He grew them up under strict laws, both dietary and moral. They were like Mary. Hail, Mary. In the Holy Qur'an, the angels came to Mary and told her, *"Mary, we have* chosen you above all women, and we have purified you. So be obedient to your Lord and humble yourself and bow down with those who bow down." This is very profound.

The angel said to Mary, "Mary, surely Allah (God) gives you good news with a word from Him of one whose name is the Messiah, Jesus, son of Mary, worthy of regard in this world and the Hereafter. And he will speak to the people when in the cradle and when of old age. And he will be one of the good ones." Mary said, "How can I have a child, and no man has yet touched me? I have not been unchaste." Allah (God) said, "Even so, Allah (God) creates what He pleases, and when He decrees a matter, He only says to it, be, and it is."

The Holy Qur'an says, "Allah (God) sent to Mary His Spirit, and it appeared unto her in the form of a well-made man." Mary knew she had not been unchaste, but a man came to Mary with God's Spirit in him. Brothers, preachers, and teachers, whenever you are in this position where you articulate the Words of Allah (God), women will love you. They cannot help themselves. They are not in love with your physical form.

They are in love with the God in you that affects them. They think it is you, but it is deeper than you physically—your eyes, your hair. It is God. That is why preachers and teachers fall victim to the law because they do not know, like a father, how to handle the adoration of women without seeking to become familiar with them in a cheap and filthy way.

That is the test of us as men. A strong man is a man who can tell a woman to save herself for the right man when he comes along. It takes a strong man to do that. We must be stronger men.

38
A Model of Motherhood

There is something personal in my life that my mother shared with me a few years ago. My mother would ask me every day to forgive her. I asked her for what, and she said she did not want me and tried to kill me in the womb. Allah (God) would not permit her to do it. She wanted to take the life of the child growing in her womb because it would have meant trouble.

Just like some of you know that an affair that leads to the birth of a child or a pregnancy, you are afraid of the consequences. Out of fear of the consequences, you think of murder. When they ask you, what is the face of a murderer, murderers look just like you and me. Look in the mirror. You are capable of murder. The circumstances just have to be right, and we will commit the act because you have been doing it, rehearsing it, over and over again.

I wondered to myself why it was so easy for me to reject myself. I do not have any pictures of myself in my house. Things have been written about me that you could stack up from when I was a little boy. I do not have any of them. If my mother had not kept the record, I would not know where it is. I have made recordings and do not know where the masters are. There is something about self-rejection and self-negation.

When I met Malcolm X, I met the first man in my life because Malcolm touched me. The Honorable Elijah Muhammad converted me, but Malcolm was my teacher. I fell in love with Malcolm because Malcolm was the strong man I always wished I could be. So, to deny myself, I became him. It is a part of murder. This is why there is so much imitation. Nobody wants to be who and what God made them.

When I met the Honorable Elijah Muhammad and got closer to him, I wanted to be Elijah Muhammad because there was nothing to me. All the time, I was murdering myself. It was not my fault as such. I was programmed from the womb to do this.

In rebuilding the Nation of Islam, I traveled this country almost killing myself, speaking in city after city, night after night. Taking honorariums that colleges would give me, I bought The Final Call building. I did it. I did not ask the Believers to give me anything, and I did not put my name on it anywhere. It belongs to the Believers. I want you to understand yourself and start looking into yourself and discover who you are and how to correct the condition that was in the womb.

I mortgaged my home and started *The Final Call* newspaper, Final Call tapes, and Final Call records. Any accountant can check the record: Farrakhan has not profited a dime. From *The Final Call*, I have paid the salaries of workers, and I have never taken a salary for myself.

Seven years later, when I moved from New York, they thought I had ripped off the Believers, and all I moved was two truckloads of furniture. After 20 years of labor and an automobile, that was all I could say was mine. As a man 42 years old, working 20 years for the Nation, I only had $7,000 to my name. I have taken abuse that only a fool or a man of God would take and never fought back, though I knew what people were thinking about me.

It is the womb. Prepared from the womb to die for a people, I was a man bringing to the Messenger $150 to $350,000 a month. My salary at the top in New York was $300 a week. I never handled any money. They paid me my top salary. Think about a man delivering $300,000 a month to the Nation, and his salary is $1,200 a month.

When the home was bought in New Rochelle—a $90,000 home that's now worth over a quarter of a million dollars—my name was not put on the deed. It belongs to the Believers. I am building a $2 million restaurant in Chicago—my name is not on the deed. It belongs to the Believers. I got the $5 million loan from Qadhafi and set up P.O.W.E.R., and my name is nowhere on the deed. It is the Nation. Why?

My children do not benefit because I was never trained from the womb to think anything of myself. Any action of mine that you thought was of arrogance and self-conceit was only a show to hide a deep-seated feeling of inferiority that came from self-negation that started from the womb.

Allah (God), in His Infinite Mercy, knows how to use a defective thing and make it something of value to show you that we can overturn the conditioning of the womb with the right kind of heart and the right kind of will to struggle. Whatever marks a child in the womb sticks with the child. It is a wonder that my children love me because I neglected them for the Nation. It is a wonder that my wife loves me.

The Honorable Elijah Muhammad said, *"Go. Allah (God) will look out for your family."* If Allah (God) did not look out for my family, I would not have one because self-negation does not end in the womb. When a woman does not think anything of herself and produces a child, she does not think enough of that child because the child was formed from what she thinks about herself.

Our children suffer because of women who do not want them and fathers who do not care whether they live or die. We must change this thing and turn it all around. Change is not going to happen unless women commit themselves. The Black woman must rise to the occasion, not just to save her people but to save the whole of humanity.

39
Direction on Nurturing

When a woman becomes pregnant, it is good news, but how you handle it from that point on is key. You do not make her feel unwanted because she is getting out of shape. The most beautiful creature you could see is a woman giving birth or developing life within her. So, you make over her.

Do not ever let her get a thought of dejection or rejection. Make her feel that she is loved and wanted and that she is going to do a great thing for humanity. During the time of your pregnancy, stay away from anger. Stay away from these filthy movies. Stay away from foolish television shows. Feed your mind wisdom and start talking to this infant while it is forming.

The first verse of the Holy Qur'an says, "Read in the name of your Lord." It is in the Chapter called "Al-Alaq," The Clot. When the baby is just a clot, start reading the Words of Allah to it. It is in a bag of water, and sound is traveling. Just like the White man can take a sound picture [ultrasound] and tell you what is going on in the womb, you can put something good in the womb with sound. Talk to your child.

Read to it while it is being formed. Read the Holy Qur'an to it. Mothers, stay in prayer, constantly reciting the attributes of Allah. When you keep saying these attributes, you impress them on the mind of your child in which the brain is being formed.

When your baby comes at the end of nine months, do not give the baby a cow's udder to suck on. Give that baby your breasts. Do not say you are too busy. You are never that busy. If you are not too busy to lay down and conceive the child, you are not too busy to feed it properly. Similac is not better for your baby than breast milk. Some women are so concerned about losing the form of their breasts that they would rather get rid of the milk than nurse the baby. That baby sucking on the breast is what preserves the form of the breasts.

You cannot beat God. His Nature is perfect. When you feed your baby formula, you stop bonding with the baby and stop passing the chemistry of your thinking to your baby. If we give a natural-born liar truth serum, he starts telling the truth when they ask the liar questions because there is a chemical in the serum.

Truth is chemistry. The reaction of truth is a chemical reaction. Fear is a chemical reaction. Hatred, envy, and jealousy are all chemical reactions. Love, mercy, truth, and goodness are also chemical reactions. If you want your baby to grow truthfully and properly, put it on your breasts. Eat good, think good, and feed that energy into your baby as it bonds itself to you.

When the weaning takes place, and you wean it away from you, you will have a mental giant growing. You cannot take that mental giant and put him in the White man's schools. If you are trying to produce a god, do not put God into the hands of Satan. It is better to go to jail fighting to teach your child at home than to make a god and then put it into the hands of an enemy who will teach your children against the value of themselves.

40
Let Us Make A Better People

We can overturn the conditioning of the womb with the Help of God. There is not one of us who cannot overturn any condition present in the womb. Mary, it is up to you. The future is in your hands. I appeal to you—produce a little messiah to help erase the condition of Lenox Avenue and 125th Street. Produce a child born from your womb to make a difference in how we live and execute life.

Girls who are not yet married, as my mother used to say, "Close your pocketbook. Do not open it up for no robber." Keep yourself together. Do not let any man make merchandise out of you. You are a sacred woman. That is why Prophet Muhammad (peace be upon him) wanted the woman in the house, not because he wanted to oppress women. When you have something sacred or of value, you do not put your valuables where thieves can rob them from you. Put your woman in a safe place.

It is on our women to make a better people. Think about how sacred you are and think about your womb. It is a gift of God. Think about how you assist God in the creation of human life. Do not let anything disgrace the beauty of this womb.

Brothers, sit down with your wife and tell her you have been a fool. Tell her you have not been yourself and you want to try again. Tell her you want to renew your love, renew your vows, and renew your commitment to each other like it was in the beginning. Let love and passion fill your embrace. Then, should you want to plan it like a scientist, say, "Let us bring one into the world that will tear Satan's kingdom down. Let us bring one into the world like Jesus." After you both agree, set the time of conception.

Give yourselves nine months or even a year to clean up your bodies and minds. Put the best foods in your bodies and go back to "How to Eat to Live." Then, make a child for God. When you find out life is conceived in your womb, give it to the Creator and ask Him to accept it from you.

I guarantee you that 20 to 25 years from now, White people will wonder what happened to change the Black community. They will see that Black women gave birth to gods, which is why their world is coming down. They will recognize that Black people started saying "Hail Mary" to the Black woman and filled her full of grace.

Blessed is that Black woman and blessed is the fruit of her womb: Jesus.

ABOUT THE FINAL CALL FOUNDATION

Final Call Foundation

The Final Call Foundation was established in 2021 with the purpose to support raising awareness, preserving, researching, and amplifying the public works and personal history of the Honorable Minister Louis Farrakhan in the uplift of all humanity.

Follow us: 🅕 🅞 @finalcallfoundation 🅣 @FCFcharity
Visit The Final Call Foundation Amazon Author Page for release updates

Available Titles

Sarah: Five Notes on a Woman's Prayer over Her Pregnancy

A study of the Biblical matriarch of the Children of Israel and Mother Summayyah Farrakhan of the Nation of Islam

A Demonstration of Love

A special collection of articles and editorials

Upcoming Titles

7 More Speeches by the Honorable Minister Louis Farrakhan

On the Sacredness of The Female

A Reason to Unite

Hurricane Katrina and the Millions More Movement

ABOUT THE EDITOR

Dora Muhammad is an artist, author, and advocate. She served as editor-in-chief of *The Final Call* Newspaper from 2003-2006. In 2010, she founded The AWARE Project, a multimedia vehicle for advocacy on issues relative to women's awareness, engagement, rights, empowerment, and advancement. In 2018, she developed the heath equity program at the Virginia Interfaith Center for Public Policy, which she still spearheads along with her role as the center's Engagement Director. She earned a Bachelor of Arts in Journalism and Documentary Photography, with a concentration in Magazine Production and completed her photography thesis at Dartington School of the Arts in Devon, England. She worked as an arts administrator for Autograph-ABP (Association of Black Photographers) while studying International Law and Human Rights at the University of London. Dora earned her Master of Public Administration and has extensive work in government relations and public policy formation. A daughter of Indo-Caribbean immigrant parents, Dora is a native New Yorker who resides in Northern Virginia. She currently serves as the executive director of The Final Call Foundation.

Visit the Dora Muhammad and AWARE Project Amazon Author Pages for more information and updates on the catalog of her books.

Made in the USA
Columbia, SC
08 December 2022

73016200R00072